T5-BAR-992

Business and Democracy

Centre for Development and Enterprise,
South Africa
Institute for the Study of Economic Culture,
Boston University

Business and Democracy

Cohabitation or Contradiction?

Edited by
Ann Bernstein
and
Peter L. Berger

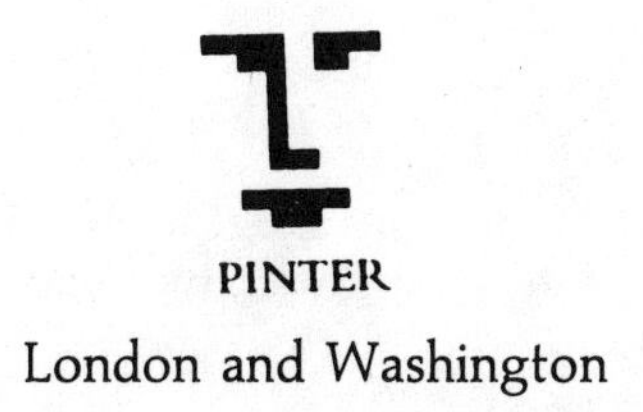

London and Washington

PINTER
A Cassell imprint
Wellington House, 125 Strand, London WC2R 0BB
PO Box 605, Herndon, Virginia 20172

First published 1998

British Library Cataloguing in Publication Data
A catalogue record for this book is available from the British Library
ISBN 1–85567–498–X

Library of Congress Cataloging-in-Publication Data
Business and democracy: cohabitation or contradiction? / edited by
Ann Bernstein and Peter L. Berger.
p. cm.
Includes bibliographical references (p.) and index.
ISBN 1–85567–498–X
1. Industrial policy. 2. Business and politics—Cross-cultural studies. 3. Democracy. 4. Capitalism. I. Bernstein, Ann. II. Berger, Peter L.
HD3611.B93 1997
338.9—dc21 97–11792
CIP

Typeset by BookEns Ltd, Royston, Herts.
Printed and bound in Great Britain by Bookcraft (Bath) Ltd,
Midsomer Norton, Somerset

Contents

Appendices

Contributors

Peter L. Berger is director of the Institute for the Study of Economic Culture at Boston University, and professor of sociology at the same university. He was previously professor of sociology at Rutgers University and at Boston College. He has written a number of groundbreaking books, including *The Capitalist Revolution, The Social Construction of Reality, Invitation to Sociology, Pyramids of Sacrifice: political ethics and social change* and *The Homeless Mind.* A former United States representative to the United Nations Working Group on the Right to Development, Professor Berger has been awarded honorary doctorates by Loyola University, Wagner College and the University of Notre Dame.

Ann Bernstein is the founder and executive director of the Centre for Development and Enterprise, an independent policy think-tank based in South Africa. From 1989 to 1995 she was an executive director of the Urban Foundation, a privately funded development and policy research organization, and head of its Urbanization Unit and then its Development Strategy and Policy Unit. Acknowledged as one of South Africa's leading development experts, she writes regularly for journals and newspapers on a wide range of socio-economic and political issues.

Richard F. Doner is associate professor of political science at Emory University. He has written widely on business issues, particularly in Japan, East Asia and the Pacific Rim, as well as on business and the state in developing countries.

R.M. (Bobby) Godsell is chair and chief executive officer of Anglogold, previously the gold and uranium division of the Anglo American Corporation of South Africa, and a director of the corporation. He has played an active role in business co-ordinating bodies, and has written widely on key political and social issues in South Africa.

Michael O'Dowd, now retired, was an executive director of the Anglo American Corporation of South Africa, and chair of the Anglo American and De Beers Group Chairman's Fund. He still chairs the Free Market Foundation. He has served on the boards and councils of numerous educational institutions. He has received honorary doctorates from the University of Natal, the University of the Witwatersrand and Rhodes University. He is the author of several books on issues surrounding economic growth and development in history.

Gustav F. Papanek is president of the Boston Institute for Developing Economies, and professor emeritus of economics at Boston University. He formerly directed what is now the Harvard Institute for International Development and chaired the Economics Department at Boston University. He has headed advisory groups to the governments of Indonesia and Pakistan, and has served as consultant to numerous governments and donor organizations. One of the world's leading development economists, he has written extensively on economics and development. Recent publications include 'The effect of government intervention on growth and equity: lessons from Southern Asia', in L. Putterman and D. Rueschemeyer (eds) *State and Market Development: Synergy or Rivalry*, and *Development Strategy, Growth, Equity and the Political Process in Southern Asia*.

S. Gordon Redding is affiliate professor of Asian business at the INSEAD Euro Asia Centre in Fontainebleau, France. He is also emeritus professor of management studies at the University of Hong Kong, visiting professor at the Manchester Business School and senior associate at the Judge Institute, Cambridge. He spent 24 years in Asia teaching and researching comparative management, his principal work being *The Spirit of Chinese Capitalism*. He has retained strong connections with the Institute for the Study of Economic Culture at Boston University, and continues to research alternative systems of capitalism, especially in the Asian context.

Ben Ross Schneider is associate professor of political science at Northwestern University. A former associate editor of *World Politics*, and director of the International Studies Program of the Centre of International Studies at Princeton University, he has written widely on business-related issues, development and democratic consolidation.

Myron Weiner is Ford International Professor of Political Science at the Massachusetts Institute of Technology (MIT), and a former director of MIT's Centre for International Studies. He is the author/editor of numerous books, including *The Child and the State in India: child labour* *and education policy in comparative perspective, The Global Migration Crisis: challenge to states and to human rights, Threatened Peoples, Threatened Borders: world migration and US policy, International Migration and Security* and *The New Geopolitics of Central Asia and its Borderlands.* Professor Weiner has taught or held research appointments at Princeton University, the University of Chicago, Harvard University, Delhi University, Hebrew University, the University of Paris, and Balliol College at Oxford.

Ernest J. Wilson III is director of the Centre for International Development and Conflict Management at the University of Maryland, and associate professor in government and politics and African-American studies at the same university. He is a former deputy director of the Global Information Infrastructure Commission, based in Washington, and director of the Policy and Planning Unit of the United States Information Agency. He has written widely on transformation and restructuring public–private sector relations in Africa.

APPENDICES

Alfredo Pastor Bodmer is professor of economics at the Instituto de Estudios Superiores de la Empresa in Barcelona, Spain, as well as the University of Barcelona.

Carlos Elizondo is a political scientist attached to the Centro de Investigacion y Docencia Economicas in Mexico City, Mexico.

Robert W. Hefner is professor of anthropology at Boston University, and associate director of its Institute for the Study of Economic Culture.

Blanca Heredia is a political scientist attached to the Instituto Tecnologico Autonomo de Mexico in Mexico City, Mexico.

Laura L. Nash is senior research co-ordinator at the Institute for the Study of Economic Culture at Boston University, and teaches business ethics and corporate culture at its School of Management and School of Theology.

Adebayo O. Olukoshi is attached to the Nigerian Institute of International Affairs in Lagos, Nigeria.

Jordi Solé Tristán is a director of the Family Enterprise Institute in Barcelona, Spain.

Bernardo M. Villegas is dean of the school of economics of the University of Asia and the Pacific in Manila, the Philippines.

Preface

Over the past few years, the Institute for the Study of Economic Culture at Boston University, directed by Professor Peter Berger, and the Centre for Development and Enterprise in South Africa, directed by Ann Bernstein, together with Bobby Godsell of the Anglo American Corporation of South Africa, have undertaken a cross-national study of the role of business in transitions to democracy and in socio-economic development.

The project had its origins in the early 1990s during a series of conversations between Bobby Godsell, Peter Berger and Ann Bernstein which began in Boston and Johannesburg and continued in London, Montreal and Amsterdam. Gradually the ideas developed, differences were narrowed and a common perspective began to emerge. In London and Montreal the conversations were expanded to include the authors of the papers included in this book (and some others); the emerging perspective on business was considerably deepened by these meetings.

Eventually, papers were produced on several interrelated themes: business and nineteenth-century transitions to democracy; business in ethnically divided countries; business and economic growth; business and civil society; and business associations in developing countries. These papers are included in this ground-breaking book. Besides these, studies were produced of Mexico, Spain, Indonesia, the Philippines, Nigeria and South Africa, augmented by an analysis of the racial transition in one city: Atlanta, Georgia. Extracts from some of these country papers appear as appendices.

The assistance of Riaan de Villiers, as well as Judith Hudson of the Centre for Development and Enterprise, in editing this book and co-ordinating its production is gratefully acknowledged.

Ann Bernstein

Introduction: business and democracy
Cohabitation or contradiction?

Ann Bernstein, Peter L. Berger and Bobby Godsell

It is significant that the current literature on business is so thin with respect to business as a social actor. The existing literature covers a number of distinct and limited areas: the organization of the firm; corporate responsibility or social investment activities of the corporation; the growth and influence of multinationals, most often from a purely business economics or Marxist perspective; and studies of the particularities of business–state relationships in selected countries.

Business as an activity, a concept and a social actor has been remarkably under-explored. Little appears to have been written on the general role and sociology of business in society. Not only does this leave business actors with little guidance in coping with rapidly changing social and political contexts; it also leaves the field wide open for other interests in society to caricature business as a concept or activity, or individual business people.

An important part of the context in which business finds itself today worldwide is the situation brought about by the collapse of communism, both as a system of government and as a persuasive ideology. For the moment, at least, there is widespread consensus that there is no viable alternative to a market economy. This has led to a much more positive attitude to business than would have been imaginable even a few years ago. It has also increased the attention given and demands placed on business from many different quarters.

The purpose of this project has been to initiate the process of thinking about business as a social actor, and in so doing to canvass the strategic implications of this for business actors. The exploratory nature of the work should be appreciated.

Although the project has dealt with business as an activity, and a number of conclusions will clearly apply to the entire business sector in any society, the major focus of the work has been on big business. This is not to deny the importance of small and medium-sized enterprises in industrialized and developing countries, but it is a reflection of the inevitable limitations of this type of relatively short-term, cross-national, comparative project, especially at this early stage of what we believe is a major conceptual reassessment.

Who is business?

The term 'business' is used very loosely in public discourse. It can be used to refer to two different entities:

- The firm – the category of individuals and organizations who are engaged in the production of goods and services for profit. The description of 'the firm' spans a spectrum from multinational corporations to the one-person enterprise.
- The business organization – the voluntary association of a number of firms into chambers of commerce and industry that could represent sectors (e.g. clothing), geographic regions or businesses within the country as a whole. Business organizations are very different from firms. Overwhelmingly, they operate on a non-profit basis and are funded by their member firms in exchange for the provision of services to those members. The origin and independence of business associations is an important area of difference between them. In some countries, these associations are created by their individual business members precisely to enable collective action, notwithstanding competing interests. As such, these bodies generally act with a longer-term sense of interests. They are also forced both by their character and the environment in which they act to articulate and justify their interests in terms of a broader public interest, rather than only in terms of market share or profitability. In other countries, business associations are not independent organizations funded by and accountable to their members, but bodies created by and dependent on the state in one way or another, and capable of differing degrees of autonomous action.

  Often, and misleadingly, the term 'business' is used to describe the activities or views of a vaguely defined collectivity of 'tycoons' – the owners and executives of the largest business groups.

Besides these analytical distinctions, there are three other factors that need to be taken into consideration when using the term 'business'. The first concerns ethnicity. In most of the ethnically divided societies of the world, corporations and retail businesses are owned and managed by individuals belonging to an ethnic minority. This generally means that the leading business associations will also be dominated by that ethnic minority, although it is likely that there will be business associations of the ethnic majority as well.

The second factor concerns size. The vast majority of firms and business corporations throughout the world are small, and yet the power, influence and number of people employed in the large corporations often dwarf anything else. It is frequently important to know whether one is referring to large or small businesses when using the term 'business'.

The third factor concerns ownership, and whether or not the business is owned and controlled by permanent residents of a particular country or by foreigners.

All the research done for this project has shown not only the diverse meanings of the term 'business', but also the rather different realities of the business sector in different societies. In each case, the answer to the question 'Who is business?' differed. What became strikingly clear is that any attempt to think about, understand or assess the role of business as an undifferentiated and undefined whole was inevitably misleading and profoundly unhelpful. In every society, it is important to see and think about the entire business sector, and not equate business in that country with only one part of what is generally a multifaceted and complex set of individuals, organizations and interests.

Having made all these distinctions, it will be noticed that we continue to use the generic term 'business' throughout the rest of this chapter. Wherever possible we do indicate the precise meaning of business that we are referring to, but often it is only possible to refer in very general terms to the business sector as a whole.

Business in society

The impact of business on society

There are unintended consequences of 'doing business'. In the course of their normal functions in the marketplace, individual companies have unexpected effects on the wider society. The normal economic activity of firms has three extra-economic consequences:

A 'thickening' of civil society

Through an examination of the role that international corporations are playing in economic change and modernization in mainland China, research for this project clearly illustrates the remarkable and profound effects of market processes on broader social structures. The research examined, as an example, the process of listing a firm on a public stock exchange and the network of institutions, rules, monitoring processes, values and procedures that are necessary for such a listing to work. From this one example of a public listing, it is possible to generalize to the kind of impact that corporations are destined to have on a society such as China and have already had on many other developing countries. It could be stated thus: a large multinational corporation needs certainty in order to invest; providing this certainty requires rules and standards; rules and standards require the means to create, monitor and maintain them; evolving, monitoring and maintaining rules and standards require institutions and associations; institutions and associations require independent individuals/professionals and evaluation; this in turn requires an independent judiciary, and information that is reliable and honest; and such information requires some form of open, free media and public debate.

Thus it can be argued that unintentionally normal business activity demands, requires and in turn creates a 'thickening web' of institutions, organizations, self-regulating mechanisms and professionals that comprise important components of civil society outside the state. (See Chapter 3 by Professor Gordon Redding: The impact of multinationals on the 'thickening' of civil society: current developments in the economy of China.)

Propelling the pressures for modernization

Through its activities – based on rationality and functionality – business reflects, creates and promotes new values, attitudes and opportunities. When a modern factory is superimposed upon a traditional society, this 'island of modernity' undermines traditional ideas of the group or tribe, inherited patterns of succession and promotion, and acceptance of age-old realities and destinies. Where two factories are each producing the same product and competing with each other, the modernizing implications multiply – from encouraging an ethos and right to individual choice and competition between alternatives versus a passive acceptance of fate, and so on.

On a larger scale, the international scope of modern economic activity, from trade to finance to consumption, opens up previously closed societies or communities to a wider world that inevitably challenges previous norms and ideas. Thus we would argue that business plays an important role in the modernization and individualization of societies. The term individualization should not be misunderstood. Business, by the way it operates, rewards individual initiative and ambition, and allows economically successful individuals to free themselves from some ancient shackles of family, village or tribe. In this sense it also fosters the emancipation of women from traditional roles of dependency. This does not imply, however, that business must necessarily be based upon or promote Western-style individualism – that is, individualism in the sense of a strong belief in the autonomy of the individual and of her/his rights *vis-à-vis* the community. The successful capitalist economies of East and South East Asia have shown that, at least in the early stages of modern economic growth, business can flourish on the basis of a strongly communitarian, non-individualistic ethic. It remains to be seen whether, in the longer run, successful capitalism will eventually generate pressures toward individualism in the Western sense.

Unleashing democratizing pressures

The business sector generally, and enterprises individually, function as alternative centres of power, influence and resources to those of the state. Business, by dint of its existence outside an undemocratic state (or within a democratic state), can contribute to greater pluralism and diversity in a society, thus strengthening the pressures for democratization. The workplace can function as a form of refuge (albeit sometimes an imperfect one) from the long reach of the authoritarian state. Business can help to open up new spaces for social and political participation through its support of opposition political parties, non-governmental organizations, community groups or development agencies. Business or their think-tanks can expand the repertoire of policy options and approaches to social change available in a society.

Business leaders and associations can form important poles of opposition to prevailing norms or policies through lending their personal and corporate prestige, status and social standing to different, sometimes unpopular, ideas. And through business exposure to a larger international community of ideas, institutions and personal contacts, the business sector contributes to challenging the 'uniqueness of this country' argument often used to justify authoritarian practices in one society when other societies are democratic. Thus business, by dint of its existence outside state-created organizations, can contribute to greater pluralism and diversity in a society, thereby strengthening the pressures for democratization.

To say that business creates democratizing pressures does not necessarily imply that successful capitalism will inevitably lead to democracy. Impressive capitalist achievements are possible under non-democratic regimes, as in imperial Germany and Meiji Japan. It is not clear that there was anything inevitable about the democratic developments in either country before democracy was imposed on them by force in the wake of World War II. While there are many cases in recent history where capitalist success had led to a process of democratization – Spain, Chile,

South Korea, Taiwan – it remains to be seen whether in other cases this process cannot be avoided.

In recent years there has been much talk about an Asian model of capitalism that supposedly rejects Western notions of democracy. Lee Kuan Yew, the former prime minister of Singapore, has been an eloquent spokesman for this point of view, and it could be said that the present regime in China is conducting a huge experiment to test this hypothesis. What we are arguing is not that democracy is the inevitable outcome of successful capitalist development, but that such development is a necessary prerequisite of democracy in the contemporary world. And that even if a society falls short of full-scale political democracy, business acts, mostly inadvertently, to modify authoritarian structures and create institutional processes that are in principle conducive to democracy. We are also saying that authoritarian regimes rarely meet the conditions under which business can optimally flourish.

In many ways, a most important and fundamental contribution that business makes to a society is through these three spheres of mainly unintended or incidental consequences of its normal activities – a 'thickening' of civil society; the promotion of modernization; and the unleashing of democratizing pressures. Business is therefore in a profound sense a constant agent of social change.

This idea is rather different from the notion of business as a pillar of the status quo, or business as a social actor that does nothing at all about social change. Thus it can be said that economic rationality inadvertently leads to individualization and institutions of civil society, and they in turn inadvertently facilitate democracy. In this sense, the marketplace, in its capital-raising, skills-allocating and goods-trading sense, is a stalking horse for democracy.

The role of business in transitions to democracy

What intentional roles can business play during a society's transition to democracy? Firstly, business can play a role as a source of policy generation. During the time that old organs of policy formation become ineffective, and before new rulers are either willing or able to address issues of governance, business can act. It can formulate desirable goals for the new political order. It can begin to elaborate appropriate means of achieving these goals. Many examples exist of how international business and economic organizations have played this role in recent years. The role of bodies such as the International Monetary Fund (IMF), the World Bank and non-governmental organizations (NGOs) such as the World Economic Forum, the International Chamber of Commerce and private consulting agencies have all played a role in defining economic policy goals for nations in transition to democracy.

Multinational corporations have also played important roles in this regard. They often have the leverage of making both substantially and symbolically important new investments in a society, in exchange for compliance with policy goals.

While international actors have been highly influential with regard to policy goals, they have been less effective in defining and sustaining the means to achieve these goals. Here the greater responsibility rests on the shoulders of domestic business, and for two reasons. Firstly, policy implementation requires detailed knowledge of domestic economic realities. Thus, while the IMF may encourage an emerging political elite to embrace the principle of trade liberalization, only domestic business can help this elite to devise a practical programme of reduced levels of trade protection and the industrial restructuring which must accompany this. Secondly, and probably more crucially, sober economic policies will only be maintained during a transition to democracy if they are accompanied by adequate levels of development. Otherwise the pain that such sober policies generally require will become politically unbearable. This reality, or rather imperative, require business to play a developmental role.

This role has at least three critical aspects. Business must help define the main goals of development. Which aspects of the present social reality must be targeted for change? Housing? Health care? Employment? Secondly, business must help to fashion specific plans consistent with the reality constraints, to achieve positive change in these areas. Thirdly, business will often have to participate in creating the institutional capacity to ensure the effective implementation of these plans.

The issue of institutional capacity is a most important one. During political transition, the old order has the capacity to get things done, but lacks the legitimacy to share the burden of development with the intended beneficiaries. On the other hand, the aspirant new leaders, while they have an insight into popular aspirations and the legitimacy to make co-demands on many communities, lack both resource and organizational capacity. It is in such conditions of a legitimacy/capacity standoff that business can play both a facilitative and an instrumental role.

South Africa's transition from apartheid to non-racial democracy provides some examples of this democratic institution-building role. Business played a distinctive role in negotiating and implementing a National Peace Accord, aimed at addressing the high levels of political violence. Probably more significant than the national role in negotiating the accord was the role business played in creating the new institutions needed to implement it. Peace committees functioned at national, regional and local levels where business was effectively involved. Although this accord and its social machinery failed to reduce violence significantly, the level of violence that would have been experienced in its absence is worth contemplating.

Nevertheless, in many communities the local peace committees represented a first attempt at creating 'a common society' where the mandated representatives of contending organizations met regularly to try through reason and debate to resolve conflict.

Business played an important role with respect to South Africa's first democratic election. Here, precisely because of legitimacy problems, a new institution was created to design and manage an election for 20 million mainly first-time voters. The capacity problems of this agency are well known to all South Africans, and were probably readily apparent to outside observers. What is less well known is the extensive role played by business in enfranchising millions of voters in their workplaces; running voter education programmes for virtually all formally employed people; running important parts of the election machinery, including voter stations; and intervening at critical moments when both the election itself and vote counting threatened to collapse.

Business – an important social actor

Whether it likes it or not, business is a powerful social actor. Its actions have consequences in the public arena, its views influence the political and policy debate, and its very existence and the terms of that existence are subjects of debate and controversy.

It is in the interests of the corporation and the business sector as a whole to become more self-conscious social actors. Both the individual firm and the voluntary business association need to think hard and strategically about their role in society, and their relationships with government and others. To do anything else is counterproductive. If business acts as though it operates in a fairly self-contained market cocoon, only consciously stepping out when its interests are directly and very obviously threatened, it allows others to project their understandings, views, prejudices and knowledge (or ignorance) of business on to the public understanding of business as a social actor. And the public perception of business as shaped by others has consequences for actions that are taken by government and other social forces. The alternative is that business adopts a much more conscious approach to itself as an actor in society: a social actor which should think about its key interests, how it is trying to achieve those interests, how it is perceived in fighting for those interests, and how those interests coincide with those of others in the society.

In developing societies in particular, with the enormous constraints that affect other interests in those societies (in terms of resources, capacity, ingenuity, confidence and innovation) – even the most powerful actor in such societies, the state – business has enormous advantages in the public debate for influence and impact. Business has resources (in whatever way it chooses to operate socially – as individual large firms or as a collectivity), it has the capacity to get things done, it has the wherewithal to hire the skills that it needs. If business were to assess its strategic advantages and disadvantages in the public arena, then business would be able to play a more aggressive and effective role in influencing public policy and political perceptions in ways that favour economic growth and a market economy. There is no objective reason why business should have to be on the defensive in the social arena. There is no need for business to wait for hostile forces to amass support for anti-market views, and only then react in a defensive way.

What is required is a clear perception of common business interests, the organizational mechanisms to define and agree those common interests, and the strategies (subtle, sophisticated and nuanced) to promote them.

The impact of society (especially a democratic society) on business

We have canvassed the impacts – especially the unintended impacts – of business on society. How do the influences work the other way?

It is in the nature of a capitalist business organization – whether an individual enterprise, or a collection of such enterprises – to be in many ways self-contained. The business enterprise raises its own capital, designs its own production processes, and defines and services its own market. In less developed and generally undemocratic societies, it is likely to become an island unto itself. Where political power is exercised feudally, or in an authoritarian context, the business organization will negotiate its existence – its right to do business, and the terms on which it is allowed to do so – with the prevailing political authority. Typically, this negotiation will take the form of a 'once-off' deal as opposed to a relationship governed by the application of general laws. Often the deal will be a private arrangement between the business concerned and the government. Frequently 'the deal' will provide the government, or officials within it, with specific benefits.

The relationship of a business entity with other social actors, in such less developed and undemocratic societies, is equally likely to take a certain form. Labour is likely to be recruited under individual contracts drawn up unilaterally by the employer. Relations with both suppliers and customers are likely to be similar. Businesses in such societies are not subject to the public spotlight of an independent and aggressively critical press. Shareholders too are likely to be compliant.

Increasing modernization, especially under democratic or democratizing circumstances, will change this. Relations with government become defined by law and regulation, with general rules requiring general compliance. Increasingly, the nature of regulation goes beyond 'simple' financial transactions. Besides taxation, companies are regulated in response to an ever widening set of public interests. Labour rights, environmental responsibilities, corporate governance, stock exchange rules, consumer rights – all these begin to impact on both the character and the conduct of the business organization.

Business is inevitably drawn into a public policy marketplace – moving from the simple 'deal' where the ruling powers allow the company the 'right to trade', to the democratizing society, where business has both constantly to legitimize itself and defend its economic, legal and other interests in the cross-play of multi-interest group politics.

Business becomes part (indeed, in developing societies a very important part) of civil society. It develops a vital interest in the rule of law and the fair application of contracts. It becomes critically interested in the fiscal and monetary policies of government; it can no longer protect its economic interests with a series of private deals with political czars, but must instead argue in the public and political marketplace for the adoption of general policies favourable to its interests.

In the process of democratization, other powerful interest groups gain space and political leverage. Organized labour, consumers and environmentalists are good examples of such groups. To ensure a broad public policy environment in which it is able to survive, business will have to engage, and often compete, with these different groups to determine the outcome of policy debates.

The research undertaken in this project has shown that business has often failed to understand its changing relationship with the forces unleashed by and within a democratizing social order. Business has been slow to define its social and political interests and is defensive, reactive and inept in promoting them. Business as a corporate citizen is often less than effective.

Interviews with business leaders in Hong Kong, and conversations with academics and journalists revealed considerable anxiety about the future of Hong Kong after the Chinese takeover, in terms of civil liberties and the future prospects for democratization with the latter. Business people, by contrast, had very little interest in this matter and came out with overtly anti-democratic views. There was a serene confidence in the economic future. One statement was made repeatedly almost in the form of a mantra: 'China will not take over Hong Kong; Hong Kong is taking over China.' The anti-democratic position was expressed succinctly by a young executive: 'We know that every society with a welfare state declines economically. We must stop the welfare state. In order to stop the welfare state, we must stop democracy.'

It is possible that these attitudes will change as the Chinese authorities continue their heavy-handed approach to Hong Kong affairs. Yet, unfortunately, it is not possible to affirm with confidence that these feisty Hong Kong businessmen are wrong in believing that they will do very well economically under the looming authoritarian circumstances. The interesting question is for how long this confidence will be warranted.

Given the propensity of the Chinese regime to make the judiciary politically subservient, and given its vulnerability to expansive corruption, it is quite possible that Hong Kong will in the not too long run become a much less plausible place in which to do business.

Business – the dilemmas of action

The business sector faces a number of dilemmas when it comes to collective and social action. The first dilemma is one of organization: how can a large number of competing entities (firms) effectively come together to promote their common interests?

The second dilemma is one of action: how do business interests/firms/organizations whose skills lie in pragmatic activities – production, marketing goods, investment, etc. – develop a sophisticated understanding of the society in which they operate, of their own interests in that society, and the most effective political strategies to promote and protect those interests? Where will the skills come from to assist business in this process?

The third dilemma is one of content: what should business actually do and say to promote its interests? What is the right strategy for growth and development in any particular country and situation?

In essence, this project is designed to start the process of unravelling some of the complexities within these dilemmas. Clearly, the particularities of a country's situation and the nature of the local business sector will form the context for dealing in practical terms with each of these dilemmas. However, the insights and analysis emerging from this project are, we believe, part of the necessary base from which these issues can be thought about and acted upon in any particular situation.

What are business interests/what does business want?

It is important to distinguish between the interests of the individual firm/corporation and those of the business sector as a whole. A further distinction relates to which interests of the firm are best handled by that firm on its own, and which interests are best handled by some or other collective representative body or business-funded organization. We also need to recognize that different sectors in business will often want or need to organize in order to protect or promote their interests against, or with, another sector of business. So, for example, a small business association will regard large corporations as targets for influence, as much as it does central government or local authorities. Importers will compete with local manufacturers. A group of businesses in one geographic area will want to protect their interests against business elsewhere. Simply put, business seeks an environment in which the profitable production of goods and services can take place. This broad purpose conceals a great deal of diversity and complexity.

Individual firms are concerned with the profitable prospects and interests of their own economic activities. In a fundamental sense, individual firms are in competition with all other firms operating in the same market, offering the same or a substitutable product or service. This notion that firms are competitive with one another must be distinguished from the idea that businesses have competing interests. Business generally has a common collective interest in a stable environment, and in a structure of governance that encourages production, service and trade, and allows competition. It is only within that framework that firms have competing interests with each other. The concept here is one of controlled competition, not competitive anarchy. All firms want a referee, and all want to influence the referee to get special treatment whenever they can.

Business organizations will have rather different concerns from individual firms. Depending on the nature of the business organization (sectoral, which sector, geographic/regional, national, etc.) it will be concerned with general threats and opportunities rather than those of an immediate commercial nature, which affect the collectivity of its membership. These will be common threats in which all the members, or at least most of them at any one time, have a shared interest. It is therefore in the interests of individual firms to co-operate with each other to ward off the threat, or to exploit the opportunity.

The larger the geographical area covered by the representative body, and the broader the range of industrial sectors represented, the more general these threats and opportunities are likely to be. For example, where a national representative business body may well back freer trade, a particular clothing company whose profitability is dependent on tariff protection is likely to oppose trade liberalization. These interest fault-lines operate not only between firms and representative bodies, but also between different business associations. For example, a representative organization whose membership is predominantly active in retail has a different set of policy interests to a body representing manufacturers. Equally, a sectoral body, such as textile manufacturers, may well have an antithetical set of interests to a body representing clothing manufacturers.

It is important to distinguish between those situations in which the individual (mainly large) enterprise can protect its long-term interests by its own actions, and those situations where only the collective action of the whole business community will provide some protection. For example, in Indonesia, if the business community were predominantly of the same ethnic group as the majority of the population, an individual large firm might reduce the risk of political or labour trouble by sensible labour policies, and becoming known as a good employer.

But when class conflicts also become ethnic conflicts, the individual firm is in a much more difficult position. In recent riots in northern Sumatra, an industrialist was killed not because he was a bad employer with particularly bad labour relations, but simply because he was a rich Chinese. In a situation like this, only the Chinese business community acting collectively could persuade the government that it prefers somewhat higher costs brought about by an independent trade union movement to the hatred that is being generated by the often quite brutal suppression of attempts of workers to organize. (See Chapter 4 by Professor Myron Weiner: Business in ethnically divided developing countries.)

In racially, ethnically, linguistically and religiously diverse societies, these factors will further distinguish business interests. Ethnic preference or prejudice may be applied to individual firms, and may affect their access to markets or capital or contracts. Where a collectivity of firms chooses to organize on a representative basis along racial, ethnic, language or religious lines, this introduces new factors. Where the ethnic character of the political elite coincides with business organization, a preferential relationship is likely to exist. Where it differs, tension may well develop.

Some firms adopt a very long-term perspective on their business, and are making decisions on that basis as much as the immediate pressures of the balance sheet. Take, for example, the development of the personal computer or investment in a large mine, both of which might only pay off in the medium to long term. Perhaps it would be better to think of the difference between the interests of the individual firm and those of the collective of firms (in one form or another) as the distinction between immediate and direct issues that affect the individual firm, and the environment in which business activity actually takes place, which is the concern of and the domain for action of the collective business organization.

Business and economic growth

It is often asserted that 'the business of business is business', and the numerous demands on business to do more than that is to misunderstand the nature of business itself. Work done during this project indicates the necessity for a more nuanced approach.

It is important to clarify the distinction between the interests of particular firms or sectors of the economy, and the pursuit of national economic growth *per se*. So, for example, it might be in the interest of exporters to devalue the currency, but when one considers the economy as a whole, it may not be the most constructive policy for economic growth.

The most natural political activity for a firm is to lobby the authorities for some or other form of intervention or special dispensation, to benefit the interests of that firm. This makes sense in terms of the short-term interests of that particular firm, but has two negative consequences. First, the intervention required by a particular firm (for example, tariff protection) is not necessarily good for other firms in that sector, firms in other sectors, or the economy as a whole. Second, the end result of this particularistic process, with each firm acting in its own self-interest, is that business can paradoxically end up as a – or even *the* – major force for an interventionist and expanded role for the state in the economy. Neither of these two consequences is good for national economic growth.

Thus, the statement that what is 'good for General Motors is good for America' is in fact not true. What is good for America or any other country is economic growth, and policies and strategies to promote that. Pursuing the interests of individual firms often results in persuading government to help that business, thus distorting the system and reducing efficiency, slowing growth and ultimately equity. What might be in the interests of a particular company at a given moment may in fact be negative for national economic growth.

What promotes growth is not the health of one firm, but a range of effectively implemented government policies that underpin and result in overall economic growth. Thus successful economic development is primarily determined by the policies of government and their effective implementation. If business wants to promote economic growth, it needs to influence the architecture of government policy. In order to do that, it needs to organize collectively.

Generally speaking, the collective interests of business in sustained economic growth will conflict with or differ from state interests when looking at the key ingredients for successful national, social and economic development. For example, disagreements will be found in the following four broad areas:

- the extent of government management or intervention in the economy;
- the role of industrial policy, and the state's capacity to 'pick winners';
- whether and how to compensate for market and state imperfections; and
- how to achieve social and development objectives.

Besides these four areas, the list will be expanded in many developing countries (and certainly South Africa) with at least four more issues:

- the ethnic composition of the business sector;
- the tension between some form of affirmative action and the integrity of purpose of institutions;
- the tension between international competitiveness and geographic, ethnic or sectoral redistribution policies; and

- the top priorities for collective national action in a situation of limited resources and expanding needs.

These are the issues around which business has to organize collectively, and define its interests. The objective has to be the formulation of business policies and strategies for national policy implementation, which in turn will form the core for a business approach to getting these ideas accepted into the political mainstream and ultimately implemented. (See Chapter 1 by Professor Gustav Papanek: Successful development and the role of business.)

Business and development

In many ways, the term 'development' has been captured by an anti-business/anti-market world view. Conceptually, it has been divided into 'good' and 'bad'. Thus, 'development' as practised by the 'development industry' is seen as 'good' development which is 'people centred', caring, respectful of communities and so on, whereas economic development is seen as 'bad', indifferent to people's needs, and something that has to be tolerated or even sometimes opposed. In a way, a line has been drawn between people development – a moral activity – and economic development – a more dubious activity. Business has allowed its activities to be excluded from 'good development', and categorized into the 'bad'. What is needed is to remove this moral distinction between the two kinds of development and demonstrate the linkages and interdependence between them.

A useful distinction can and should be drawn between growth and development. It is possible to have economic growth from which only a few people in society benefit. Development, although impossible without economic growth, has a different meaning. Essentially, development is the process in which the fruits of economic growth are used to uplift large numbers of people from great poverty to a level of relatively decent material life. We can speak of development when increasingly large numbers of people experience a dramatic upturn in their own or (at worst) their children's standard of living.

Where there have been big success stories in terms of development, these have always occurred in countries with market economies. In other words, the market economy is the necessary, but not sufficient, condition for long-lasting economic growth and development. The extent of development generated by economic growth depends on both the nature and quality of that growth, and the wisdom and efficacy of the development strategies pursued by the society as a whole and the state in particular.

At certain times in a country's history, a trade-off seems inevitable between growth and development. That is, certain social needs can only be addressed when the national resources have been created to address them. Precipitous social expenditure can destroy the growth capacity of the economy. Similarly, it should be noted that a failure to make critical selected social expenditures at the correct time can also have disastrous economic and social consequences. There are large areas of social spending that have a virtuous impact on the economy's growth capacity. This would appear to be particularly true of appropriate investments in education, training, health, infrastructure and housing.

The linkage between growth and development policies is important. If the social side of development requirements are neglected, the consequences of this neglect will have economic effects. For instance, if the majority of people do not have access to an effective basic education system, their lack of skills will hamper the development of a modern economy. Similarly, if the physical infrastructure of the cities is neglected, the time and resources absorbed by inadequate transportation will detract from the general efficiency of the economy. If these social and infrastructural needs are neglected, the stability of the prevailing regime will sooner or later come under threat. There are two consequences of that. Either the state will overcompensate and resort to populist-type policies that will absorb far too much of national resources and lead to inflation, a decline in international investment and borrowing, and thus affect economic growth detrimentally; or the state will continue to ignore the needs and rising anger of large parts of the population and thus heighten the possibility of growing instability and even a fundamental challenge to the regime.

The leaders of this challenge are unlikely to be defenders of private property, the free market or economic growth as the only basis for redistribution and greater equity. Of course, both these scenarios could also result in a return to authoritarianism and an increasing percentage of the budget being absorbed into repression, control and policing, with the inevitably negative effects of that on economic growth.

A further reason why business has a major interest in social development issues is that if government policies are adopted in this arena, which 'crowd out' the private sector, the consequences will be negative for economic growth and national development. In the majority of countries, if the state tries to deliver social services itself, the enormity of the task will necessarily entail failure, and services will fail to be provided to the vast majority of the population except for a politically well-connected minority. This result will lead to a version of one of the above scenarios.

In addition, if the state dominates and 'crowds out' the private sector in the socio-development arena, the likelihood of state intervention growing in other parts of the economy will increase. It also means that the many opportunities for private sector activity in the provision of social services, infrastructure, health care and refuse collection will be denied. This exclusion will affect the expansion of the private sector generally, and in particular close off many areas for the development and support of small business activity that could benefit disadvantaged individuals and local communities. All this will affect the growth rate, and the nature of economic development.

Business has a direct interest in the state's economic policies and their effective implementation. Business has an equal interest in the state's social and development policies. These two different but intimately interrelated areas of policy are essential for national success, and the size, scope and health of business activity are affected by the nature of state policies adopted in these two areas of social and economic policy.

If business wants to operate in a growing economy characterized by political and social stability, then business will need to act to promote government actions that are in the interests of business and its definition of growth and development. The challenge then is threefold:

- business has to develop an approach to national economic growth;
- this approach must be integrated with a business perspective on development; and
- in turn, both of these have to be marketed in the political arena and then effectively implemented by the society concerned.

So the collective interests of business dictate the need for a common vision that links growth and development; for effective public marketing, to sell this business vision of growth and development; for a strategy to achieve such growth and development by the society; and for the strategic and tactical skill to make the economically and socially necessary, politically possible.

Business and democracy

Democracy and economic growth

The critical questions concerning the relationship between business and democracy are: Is democracy in the interests of business? Does democracy facilitate growth and development, or impede these processes? Comparative experience suggests a differing relationship. Clearly, where democracy is sustained the pressures for development become unavoidable. A government that has to give account of its stewardship of power to an electorate after a four- or five-year term of office is forced to take the improvement of the voter's quality of life very seriously. The relationship with growth is more complex. The prerequisites for gaining power and managing an economy are often at odds with each other, at least in the short term.

Conversely, there is evidence to suggest that development and growth are possible in non-democratic political orders. Whatever our preferences might be (and they are certainly for democracy), it is possible to conceive of a situation in which an authoritarian regime is in the interests of business. Such a regime could only be in the interests of business and economic growth if the following conditions can reliably be met by such an undemocratic regime:

- it can really control the country and establish a stable and certain environment for a reasonable length of time;
- it implements intelligent economic and social policies. In other words, the anti-democratic regime implements economic and social policies that promote sustainable economic growth and ensure effective delivery of development to the mass of citizens;
- the institution and maintenance of such an undemocratic regime does not require a reign of terror involving widespread human rights abuses and large-scale bloodshed;
- the scale of corruption and graft in and emanating from the public sector can be and is kept within reasonable limits, to the extent that they do not affect the pace of economic growth, attack the very foundations of law and order, and destroy public faith in the institutions of state and government.

Although it is possible for these four conditions to be met simultaneously, comparative experience suggests that this rarely happens. This difficulty is exacerbated when one insists that the four conditions need to be met and sustained over a lengthy period of time. This being the case, we would argue that, sooner or later, the interests of the business sector will dictate that democracy is in fact the better option. Even in the cases where logic forces one to concede the possible benefits of an authoritarian regime for business and economic growth, these circumstances are unlikely to prevail for long, and the logic of the situation will shift towards the democratic option.

Thus, in authoritarian regimes, one can argue that business has an interest in a successful transition to democracy. This means that business needs to clarify and promote its own interest during the transition, as there is no guarantee of what the outcome of such a fundamental social transformation might be. There are two major areas of concern for the business sector.

At a time of such fundamental social change, many, if not all, of the institutions and values of the past come under scrutiny. This will apply to the values and organizations of the business sector as much as, if not more so than, any other. In many societies, the very existence of a set of economic activities based on private property and free exchange is under threat. Because business is able to adapt to different types of political regime, and needs to co-operate with the authorities in order to get things done, business is often perceived to identify with the authoritarian regime rather than the new democratic order. In this context, the interests of business as a collective class are clear. Ways must be found to legitimize and popularize business as an activity which is essential and desirable for a new democracy. The benefits of business activity for economic growth, development and democratization need to be marketed.

Periods of fundamental regime change are characterized by complex and multiple sets of actors jockeying for power and influence to shape and control the new society and its institutions. In such circumstances, business interests dictate two sets of activity, the one positive and the other defensive. On the positive side, business as a class must be clear on what kind of transition and future institutions are best for economic growth. In other words, business must play its part in an extremely fluid environment, to push as hard as possible for the kind of transitional mechanisms and policies that will promote economic growth and development. It must therefore not only promote its views on transition, but support those who share its values and basic approach.

On the defensive side, business actors need clear policies and strategies as reference points in a period of uncertainty to ensure that they are not unwittingly co-opted on to the agenda of other interests for the transition and beyond. It is quite possible for business to share a common desire for a successful transition with other actors, while at the same time differing on the most desirable and effective strategies for future economic growth and development, or the nature of a future democratic system. These differences must continually be kept in mind. Business must not fund or use its resources to strengthen its own enemies.

In a democratizing society, a business community that wishes to support growth strategies has to do so distinctively. In an authoritarian or feudal political order, business can develop close relationships and make private deals with the power elite. In a democratizing society, business must argue its case in a public marketplace of policy ideas. It must present and argue its proposed policies as being in the public good, and not merely in its own interests.

Not only must business define its interests in a different way in a democratizing society; it must also organize itself differently. In a society governed by an elected representative government, and where public policy is made through open public debate in national assemblies or councils, the most effective voice for business will be that of its representative organizations. Individual entrepreneurs from large corporations may still have influence through informal channels. However, if their views are not also presented in the public policy marketplace by credible, representative business organizations that can claim to represent a significant majority of the businesses operating in a particular sector or nationwide, they will not be able to influence the national debate.

Business and consolidating democracy

In a democracy, then, especially a newly formed and emerging democracy, business has a new kind of role to play. In essence, business has an interest in the consolidation of the new democracy and in ensuring that non-populist economic and social policies are adopted and implemented by the state. Without going into country-specific detail, we will try to spell out what this means.

With respect to national policies, it is possible to identify the 'pegs in the ground' for a business approach. In general, business should promote policies and strategies to encourage rapid economic growth and sustainable mass development while being sensitive to the political and social problems that these policies may cause in the short to medium term. This means that a business-oriented approach should:

- *Resist state-centred patronage policies*: In practice, this will mean that business must enter the public debate and expose the fallacies and dangers of such policies for the country, economic growth, the business sector and the poor.
- *Formulate and promote alternative policies* not only with respect to economic matters but also with regard to broader development issues, particularly policies that will alleviate the problems of the poor, and those most vulnerable to economic and structural changes.

The detailed policies and national development approaches that business should advocate must emphasize the following principles:

- *The importance of providing hope for the future to the majority of citizens* and their children. This can be done by selecting achievable priorities for national attention, such as basic education, health and housing; making people feel that the government and the establishment generally cares about them and their problems; and limiting corruption as much as possible.
- *Quickly expand the income-earning opportunities and productive capacity of the poor.* The state should allocate substantial funds to labour-intensive public employment projects. These projects should be used to develop needed urban and rural infrastructure; they should provide skills which can later be transferred to the formal economy; and the projects should be implemented through a decentralized and competitive approach involving communities, business, civil society and the central and local state.
- *Strengthening civil society and maximizing private sector capacity* (business,

non-government organizations, etc.) in delivery. This can be done through seeing the state as primarily an enabling and co-ordinating actor whose job it is to see that society provides certain goods and services, but not doing this itself unless absolutely necessary.

- *Emphasizing the international experience of similar economic and development challenges* to assist society to learn and adapt the lessons of that experience as quickly as possible.
- *Underlining the scale of the challenge to be met and the necessity for pragmatism* in order to achieve sustainable, countrywide results, rather than merely create new 'pockets of privilege' in a vast sea of poverty.
- Repeat again and again the *necessity for the new regime to empower individuals and communities rather than bureaucrats and politicians.*

Business and government

Superficially, it would seem as if the term 'government' is much simpler than that of business. Yet here, too, closer examination reveals a high degree of complexity. At least three distinctions must be drawn. Firstly, government has both an executive and a legislative arm. Secondly government operates in most countries on a national, regional and local level. Thirdly, within government an important distinction must be drawn between the politicians and the officials, and within the officials between career bureaucrats and those who are politically appointed.

In democratic political systems, governments exercise all the powers of the state in a way that will uphold the constitution and keep them or their party in office through one or more elections. For elected politicians, their particular electorate will define the interests which drive their immediate concerns. Thus politicians with regional rather than national electorates will tend – in the first instance – to reflect regional rather than national interests. Where politicians hold elected office (in, say, a legislative assembly) and also exercise an executive role in regional or national government, the interests of their electorate will inevitably be modified by the demands of government. At the very least, they will now have to deal with the conflicting demands of many different electorates as well as the constraints of implementation.

Government experts, technocrats and bureaucrats may once again develop quite distinct interests. They may need to develop expertise and influence that will survive the vicissitudes of electoral fashion. In particular, those employed in the executive functions of the state are likely to derive their power from this ability to make state systems work, and their mastery of bureaucratic procedure and politics. The impact of new ideas and new interests on these established highways and byways of governmental action is likely to be of decisive interest to this group.

If it is accepted that business is a social actor and that it has common interests that supersede those of individual firms, then we would argue that business interests need to rethink their relationship with government. In essence, if business interests want to influence government, then there needs to be a much greater understanding of government by the business sector, and greater clarity on the nature of the business/government relationship. It needs to be understood that government has very different imperatives to those of business. Under democratic conditions, at any rate, government is accountable in a different way and to different groups than individual businesses. Also, its 'stakeholders' will demand very different things of it than those that are asked of business.

Democracy installs an authority in government (at all levels) which is the only institution in society with the official responsibility for society as a whole, and all its members. Therefore, the relationship of the business sector with government must be underpinned by the recognition of several important realities. Firstly, that business in dealing with government is engaging with an entity whose legitimacy must be recognized if democratic order is to be preserved, and if business interests are to have any influence over it. Secondly, that the legitimacy, responsibilities and rights of those in the business sector are different from those of a democratically elected government. Thirdly, that business is one of a number of interests in a society, and that no interest group in a democracy has any legitimate claim to rights and privileges not available to every other interest. Fourthly, that it is very difficult for a government (central, regional or local) to deal with hundreds of competing firms and different views (other than at the level of favours, patronage, etc.).

Business needs to engage as a common, organized set of interests, and ensure that its views and interests are effectively communicated to government. This will require effective mechanisms for interaction within the business sector and between business and government that are appropriate to the issues on the table and to the levels of government and business that need to interact on a particular issue.

Some practical examples

All the preceding recommendations are based on three general assumptions, for which there are good empirical warrants: the first is that an overall framework exists for economic growth, one that by now is very widely accepted. (There will, of course, be debate over the strategy for its implementation, tactics, timing and so on, but the key elements of the formula are no longer in major dispute.) The second is that the application of this formula must be politically sustainable, which in a democracy or democratizing situation means that growth policies must be related, and seen to be related, to an agenda of social development. And the third is that business has a role in correlating growth and development actions, both in what it can do by itself and in what it can recommend to government.

But these assumptions are very general. The following examples are meant to illustrate the overlap of government and business actions. They were mainly inspired by the South African situation, but they can be replicated in their essential features in other developing societies.

Housing

Government proposes the policy goal of greatly increasing the housing supply for poor people. Government sees as its own proper functions the elaboration of an overall plan, as well as regional and local planning (these may of course be undertaken by different levels of government), land allocation, and zoning and building infrastructure. But government also recognizes that for both economic and political reasons it does not wish to become the major national landlord; therefore, it invites private developers and banks to help the policy by entering the 'poverty housing market'. It does so in terms of rhetoric about the 'social responsibility' of business (and also in terms of 'reparations' for alleged past misdeeds by the business elite). Should developers and banks prove reluctant to take up this invitation, government may charge them with 'red-lining', due to racial or class prejudice, and enact legislation to prevent this from continuing to occur.

Business, while acknowledging instances of prejudice, past or present, and agreeing that racial or other economically irrelevant discrimination should be outlawed, should reject the overall charge. Business should not be expected to engage in activities in which it is certain to lose money. Specifically, business should not be asked to lend money (in this case in the form of mortgages) to people who are likely not to repay the loans and whose assets (here in the form of houses) cannot be repossessed, because any attempt to do so will lead to violence.

Government may respond by offering some form of mortgage guarantees. However, these may constitute a sort of 'blank cheque' – if the guarantees are claimed with any frequency, government will be unable to meet this financial demand, will have to limit the guarantees, which in turn will create problems of allocation (whose houses will be afforded such government protection?), and may soon undermine the overall policy goal.

Government may then respond by instituting a kind of triage, differentiating between three levels of poor people: those in formal employment who can get into the commercial mortgage system on their own; those in formal employment who cannot; and the unemployed or informally employed. Government can then decide that the first group can be left to its own devices with respect to housing (which may or may not be politically difficult). The third group may be helped to sustain and in time upgrade informal housing by governmentally subsidized (private sector provided) infrastructure and services. The second group will be the most plausible target for concerted joint government/business actions, with government providing incentives (albeit through guarantees, tax relief or other means) for developers and banks to enter this sector of the housing market.

This in itself will not take care of the aforementioned problem of lending in situations of commercially unacceptable risks. Both government and business should then muster the political courage to point out that the overall housing policy will fail unless property rights are secured by a viable law and order regime. On the part of government, this will mean a plausible and highly visible application of its police powers. In other words, housing policy will have to be directly related to a policy of suppressing violence and rule by force of law. Depending on the local situation, this could be a formidable exercise, though one may expect a 'multiplication effect' from widely publicized cases of vigorous police actions that make neighbourhoods safe for the peaceful expansion of business activity (and not only in terms of housing – any business activity is undermined by a culture of lawlessness and violence). Government and business can co-operate in communicating to the public the need for suppressing violence and respecting the law.

Education

This opens up another area of policy. The term 'culture' has just been used. The overall goal here must be to substitute an 'enterprise culture' for an existing culture that devalues enterprise. Government is notoriously weak when it tries to influence culture – except in the area of education. Government and business can further co-operate in fostering education toward positive attitudes in respect of enterprise, specifically by means of 'enterprise schools'. These are likely to be opposed by various interest groups, especially from within the existing education establishment.

Such opposition can be countered by empowering parents, most of whom are likely to be much more favourably disposed than teachers to an enterprise-oriented education. Such empowerment can take different forms, in ascending order of radical change – parental participation in the running of schools, tax relief (or, for the poor, a negative tax) for parents of schoolgoing children, and educational vouchers.

Other policy areas could be selected to the ones enumerated here. The main point, though, has been made: this particular policy area cannot be successfully attacked unless economic and social agendas are continually related, and unless this nexus is made politically viable. Business, while remaining conscious of its irreducible interests, can co-operate with government at every step.

Delivery

Governments want jobs, houses, services, education and opportunities for its citizens. In order to achieve this, government wants business to assist in providing these jobs, houses, services and so on. The enormous contribution that business can make to delivery should not be underestimated, particularly in developing countries, where private firms are a very important source of capacity for managing resources and delivering. But for business to play a role in delivery there are certain preconditions that need to be met. In order to maximize business involvement, government needs to accept that:

- Firms exist in order to make a profit, and that if they cannot do so, they go out of business.
- Incentives need to be provided for business involvement in those areas of social need and delivery that are outside the more natural areas of business activity. In essence, government needs to find creative ways in which limited public sector resources can leverage greater private sector resources for delivery.
- Business and government have different strengths and weaknesses, and different roles to play.
- Business is at its best in environments of opportunity, freedom to innovate, expanding markets, and incentives to experiment and perform. Government has to be accountable for ensuring delivery to all citizens, for monitoring the quality of service provision, and for the proper accounting of public resources.

In finding the best road to a happy mix of the state's need to deliver, and the private sector's requirement to survive as businesses, certain principles are essential:

- The distinction between public resource allocation and how this money is spent is crucial.
- The state must enable and facilitate, business should implement according to state needs, and the state should monitor its efforts.
- The business sector can only play this role in a stable environment where rule by law is enforced and is the norm.
- Humility in what works in the field of social and many other areas of policy is essential. There is no one answer, and the best approach is a continual process of 'social learning' where mistakes are made, businesses fail, governments are thrown out of office, and new experiments hopefully build upon what was learnt the time before.
- Competition is accepted as a healthy and inevitable organizing principle for effective delivery. Competition will promote innovation, and help a society to learn more quickly what will work and why. This means that competition between cities and towns and different levels of

government on different approaches to how to deliver is essential. So too is competition between firms on how things can be done effectively and efficiently.

- The need to promote an entrepreneurial culture – cities, governments and individuals can all be entrepreneurial.

Government has an interest in seeing this kind of approach work, because it is the only route to mass delivery in the context of a developing society. Business has an interest in 'marketizing' service provision, infrastructure delivery and so on, as this expands markets and opportunities and thus provides enormous scope for firms to expand and grow. Finding ways in which market-based approaches to delivery can be extended into services for poor communities has benefits for those communities that can obtain training from companies, and can themselves become entrepreneurial in meeting their own needs.

Cities and towns

Governments want increased economic growth, housing, services and infrastructure delivered to millions of people. Where will all this take place?

In many developing countries growth and development will primarily occur in the cities and towns. Urban areas are the core locations in which most national economic and development policies, and local policies too, are enacted, tested and modified by reality. This means that national governments have an overriding interest in the health and efficiency of their urban sector (metropolitan areas, cities, secondary cities, towns) as the vital arena for almost all national policies, and the location of most of the country's economic growth and population.

Business (in all the meanings of the term) is primarily an urban activity, especially in today's modern world. What cities offer firms are ready-made and accessible markets, good communications, transport, services, the many benefits of agglomeration of population, business sectors, skills, innovation and so on. Therefore, business too has an interest in the efficient functioning of urban areas as arenas for investment, growth and expansion, and also as desirable places in which managers and skilled workers want to live and educate their children. Not only does business have an interest in the efficiency and liveability of a city, but this in turn is based on the political stability of the city. The efficiency and stability of urban areas will depend on the quality of national and local governance as it affects economic, social and political dynamics in cities and towns.

In the nexus of growth and development, government and business have to worry about certain core areas of concern that affect cities:

- Any country that wants to be a part of the international economy has also to think of the competitive potential of its cities and towns. Cities are continually competing with each other, both within a country and between countries. So the core question for each city and town is the competitive one: Is this city a competitive arena for economic growth? Can it hold on to the investment and businesses that it currently has, and can it attract additional new investment and entrepreneurs? Thus, government has to worry about the future of its cities in terms of their contribution to national economic goals. And national business interests also have to worry about the health and efficiency of the cities as arenas for growth and investment, and the key place in which most of their economic activities will be played out.

- This makes urban issues such as financing urban infrastructure and future development, effective local government elections and constitutional powers for cities matters of national concern to both business and government.
- The quality of urban governance is therefore critically important. National governments have a direct interest in legitimate and effective organs of local government, as the direct agents to ensure the delivery of the necessary services and processes to create and sustain effective cities and towns. National and local business interests also have an interest in these matters, and this will often involve direct intervention to facilitate this. Local government needs to mobilize the energies and commitment of key stakeholders in cities to agree on the desired future of a place, and how best to achieve it. In that process, local business is a key participant with a direct interest in that urban future, and the demands and opportunities an agreed vision provides it with.
- Here again, delivery will have to start with a strong stand on rule by law and the enforcement of those laws. So if people do not pay for services, it is impossible to think of public/private partnerships for delivering new services. This means once again that tough action by both central and local government is required if the capacity and delivery systems and ultimately commitment to stay in that city of the private sector are to be brought into play at the local level.
- National policies (trade, pricing, policing, etc.) are frequently thought about at the national and central level, with little understanding of or concern for how they will affect particular places such as cities and towns, and the business and other interests in them. Similarly, local events can affect national issues. For example, the weak condition of the financial sector in most developing countries, and particularly its difficulty in mobilizing private savings, has meant that the financing of urban investment has weighed heavily on central government. The fiscal linkage between the urban economy and the macro economy is equally important: poor local government revenue performance contributes to the consolidated national budget deficit.

Concluding remarks

Very often, business people as well as outside observers of business hold one or the other view of how business can be expected to behave in society. There is the 'hard-nosed' view that business will pursue its economic interests regardless of the social and political fallout, and that it is a sentimental illusion to expect it to do anything else. There is also the 'soft' view that holds that business people are susceptible to moral appeals, and that, in heeding such appeals, business should practise 'social responsibility' and act as 'good corporate citizens'. We have considerable difficulty in fitting ourselves into either view. We feel compelled to take a more nuanced, in-between position.

Of course, individual business people are moral beings and there are occasions when they may act as such, both in their business actions proper and in their political involvements. But insofar as they are responsible for the economic survival and success of a business enterprise, all their actions take place under quite severe constraints. The economist's view is correct to the extent that the economy is an autonomous world, following its own logic; anyone who wishes to survive and flourish in that world must act within that logic. What is more, the logic is morally neutral – it will reward the scoundrel as easily as the saint. Put differently, it is foolish to expect business people to act against their own business interests; it is equally foolish to expect business as an institution to be something that it is not, such as a morally inspired agent of social change, an efficient political machine, or a repository of intellectual wisdom.

We have tried to show that business, simply by doing what it knows how to do – generating profits for itself and its shareholders, and creating wealth for the general society – will unleash processes favouring modernization and development, and indirectly facilitate moves towards democracy. To say this is to reiterate under present-day conditions Adam Smith's seminal insight that morally laudatory consequences can follow from morally neutral actions.

We should not be misunderstood. We do not want to denigrate individuals in the business community who on occasion may undertake actions for moral reasons, even if their immediate economic interests may dictate different actions. Such individuals should be honoured. They are also rare. What is more, if they persist in acting against their own economic interest, their future is likely to be one of morally uplifting bankruptcy – which will certainly preclude their capacity to go on doing uplifting things.

This leads to a simple but far-reaching conclusion: while one should not follow the economists in believing that human beings always act out of rational self-interest, it is prudent to rely on interests rather than moral conviction if one wants to predict the behaviour of economic actors (and, incidentally, other actors as well). If nothing else, interests tend to be more long-lasting than moral enthusiasms. This is not at all to reject churches and other institutions of moral instruction making appeals to the conscience of business people. Often interests are unclear, the future is uncertain, different courses of action are possible – and then acting in response to a moral principle may well be the preferred option. One may quote Mark Twain here: 'When in doubt, do the right thing.' As a rule, though, it is the safer bet to appeal to the interests of business people rather than to their consciences.

Consequently, we have not engaged in moralizing on any of the above (though, obviously, we have moral beliefs ourselves); not in terms of helping the poor, or promoting a more just order, or fostering democracy. We have assumed that business will be motivated by its interests. We have considered various courses of action open to business on the basis of such interests, though we have found it important to make two distinctions – between the interests of individual firms or economic sectors, and the interests ('class interests', if you will) of business as a whole – and between short-term and long-term interests. We have noted with a measure of relief that despite the 'hard-nosed' flavour of our approach, its conclusions have not put undue strain on our moral beliefs. Adam Smith's 'invisible hand', perhaps surprisingly, continues to be a useful metaphor for the effects of capitalist enterprise.

Some strategic recommendations

Some concluding remarks are offered which we believe have implications for business action.

Who is 'business'?

The term 'business' is used very loosely in public discourse (and often pejoratively). It can mean at least three things: all individuals who share the activity of producing goods and services for profit (which embraces the CEO of a multinational corporation and the owners of a corner grocery); organizations whose purpose it is to protect and promote the interests of business as they see them; and a vaguely defined collectivity of 'tycoons', owners and executives of the largest business groups. The complexity of the business sector should be communicated to others in society when business people address the public.

In societies with ethnic divisions, it is dangerous for business to comprise only one ethnic group, especially when the latter is a minority and political power is in the hands of a different ethnic group which is in the majority. Efforts should be made to expand the business sector, so that the ethnic majority is a major player in the economy as well as in politics.

This will involve both activities within business organizations (in recruitment, training, and the like) and activities outside them (subcontracting to majority-owned enterprises, whether big and small, fostering business education for majority members, and the like).

Similarly, it is dangerous when the business sector of a society is dominated by foreign companies. These have a direct interest in 'indigenizing' their own local organization, but also in helping to strengthen local business enterprises. It is not in their long-term interest to do this in the form of 'crony capitalism' (doing business exclusively with, say, the relatives and friends of the government leaders) but rather to help expand the private sector of the economy in a competitive manner.

Business, a constant agent of social change

Business people are often asked what they 'are doing' to promote desirable social change, development and democracy. The implication is always that business should undertake actions specifically aimed at these processes. Fair enough. But it should be pointed out that business, by the simple fact of 'doing business', is having an important social impact – not just as a direct result of the economic growth fostered by business activity, but by 'thickening' the institutions of civil society, promoting modernity, and unleashing democratizing pressures. The marketplace in its capital-raising, skills-allocating and goods-trading sense is a 'stalking horse for democracy'.

Business and realpolitik

Business needs to think about, and deal with, different political situations in a nuanced way. In an authoritarian situation, business is primarily involved in deals with the political elite, behind closed doors. This probably cannot be avoided: however, it is not in the long-range interest of business to be perceived as a pillar of a repressive regime. Thus, business should seek distance between itself and the regime and also, wherever possible, communicate to different social actors the economic, political and social benefits of its presence in society.

In a situation of transition to democracy, it is important to realize that the very existence of private property and a market economy may be put in question as a result of the political transformation, and that generally business will have to change the way it operates in the society concerned. It is also important in such a situation that business must have its own agenda and communicate it effectively to all relevant political actors. This will require organizational (and support) mechanisms different from those with which business promoted its interests in the pre-democratic period.

In a democratic situation, the public debate becomes much more important. Business must operate as one interest group among many. It will have, once again, to be very clear about its agenda. Business will need strategies to:

- formulate sound policy proposals;
- ensure support within the key components of the business sector for these policies;
- communicate its policies effectively to different audiences;
- legitimate its right to have an agenda that is different from those of the state or others in the society; and
- ensure that its policy ideas are fully debated and considered in the public debate, and in the legislative and executive arms of government.

Business will need to show that what it wants for the country is also in the national interest. Once again the appropriate organizational and support mechanisms for this public role will have to be thought through and established.

Growth and development

While logic would suggest that business should always support economic growth, this has not always been the case. The main reason for this is that the short-term interests of an individual firm or business sector are not always identical with the long-term interests of business as a whole. Business people must carefully reflect on the way in which their activities support or fail to support economic growth, and then on how the short-term interests of some among them (say the interests of local manufacturers in import tariffs) relate to the long-term interests of all of them (say in trade liberalization).

Growth and development are closely linked, but not the same, if by development one means (what is usually meant) that large numbers of people are lifted from misery to decent standards of life. In a democratizing society, it is not enough for business to say that it fosters growth and therefore, *ipso facto*, development. Sometimes there will be conflicts between policies fostering the two goals, if only in terms of which will take precedence over a particular time span. The legitimacy of business will be strongly affected by the way in which business is perceived as caring about and helping to bring about development. Thus, business will have to reflect on how its own interests relate to possible alternatives in development strategy, and how these preferences can be communicated to government as well as to the wider public in an effective manner.

In a democratizing and democratic situation, business will have to play a public role through broadly representative organizations which make the case for certain policies in terms of broader societal concerns, and through open debate in the political marketplace. This applies both to economic policies proper (where business interests are generally reasonably clear) and also to social policies that will sooner or later impact on business. To this end, business will have to find forms of organization that transcend the division between the interests of firms and sectors on the one hand, and what might be called the collective interest of business on the other, as well as the division between short-term and long-term interests.

In shaping organizations to represent business in the context of democratic politics (where votes must be counted and coalitions put together), the relations between big, medium and small business will have to be taken into account. In many developing societies, the ethnic composition of business will also have to be considered.

Business needs a sophisticated and up-to-date understanding of the economic, political and social dynamics of the society in which it operates. It cannot always rely on other institutions (such as the media or the universities) to provide the information and policies that it needs. The media are notorious for distorting reality, usually in a pessimistic vein, in order to be sensational. The universities are often engaged in esoteric intellectual games that have no bearing on anything that goes on in the real world. And both media and universities are full of people with an anti-business animus. Business may have to establish its own mechanisms for these purposes.

Socio-economic and corporate policies

On the national level, business should favour a realistic linkage between economic (i.e. growth) and social (ie. development) policies. In both areas, these policies should be:

- anti-statist – that is, favouring the private sector (market and non-profit actors) both in the economy and in society generally;
- anti-populist – that is, eschewing unrealistic promises and revolutionary redistribution; and
- anti-corruption.

Economic policies should be consonant with international competitiveness as well as job creation. Social policies should favour the institutions of 'civil society' (that is, institutions based on voluntary association and that are non-state as well as non-profit) and the empowerment of the largest numbers of citizens (as against the creation of a dependency class and/or policies that only benefit the politically favoured few).

Bearing in mind the shortage of resources, personnel and experience in most developing societies, the fact that business tends to have more of all three than other institutions, sometimes including government, there should be considered reflection on how business capacity can be 'lent' to other sectors of society (including where appropriate/if indicated) to government. This capacity of business to 'get things done' can be very helpful in getting things to happen in a pro-business and not in a statist manner.

In terms of what has traditionally been seen as 'corporate social responsibility', the findings of this project would lead us to suggest a new look at this field:

- Business should always know what its own interests are and what it is trying to achieve with a social intervention at the community, city or regional level.
- Where business interests indicate this, similar actions to those discussed on the national level should be considered, that is, favouring development as well as growth and making business interests congruent with the interests of the wider community.
- Business will have to get involved in local debates, and seek to strengthen local institutions of civil society. It should be aware that even in ethnically homogeneous societies, the term 'community' is somewhat of a fiction. In fact, there are always diverse communities; business should be aware of and in contact with those that are politically and socially significant.
- In order to accomplish its purposes, it is not enough for business to give money; participation by senior staff is of great importance.
- Business should not assume that extra-economic issues are easy. Senior management time and effort is required in order to understand and then act effectively upon the socio-economic environment. This does not necessarily mean that business should do this itself, but that real expertise is required, and this needs to be found, funded or hired.
- Business should never fund its own enemies – i.e. people or organizations opposed to market values and to the role of corporations in society.
- Lastly, it is worthwhile for business to undertake periodically a thorough and independent evaluation of its extra-economic activities, their actual impact on society, and their continuing relationship to business interests.

The present time is one in which there is greatly diminished hostility to business in most of the world. Business-friendly policies have been multiplying in what only recently would have been considered as very unlikely places – in Eastern Europe, on the Indian subcontinent, in sub-Saharan Africa, in Latin America. And many intellectuals have given up the anti-capitalist views that held sway only a few years ago.

This is a window of opportunity for those who would like to see business take a more active role in shaping the direction of the societies in which it operates. There is no guarantee that these favourable circumstances will continue. The dislocations brought about by the highly dynamic, globalized economy is creating losers as well as winners, among nations and within national societies. The losers are very susceptible to various populist ideologies which, if successful in shaping policy, will harm or even arrest both growth and development, and will have very destructive consequences for business. There exists now a possibly unique historical moment for business as a social actor. The opportunity should not be missed.

1

Successful development and the role of business

Gustav F. Papanek

The key to a successful development strategy – for it to gain and maintain the political support of the majority of the population – is rapid, labour-intensive growth that creates strong demand for unskilled labour. The experience of the last 40 years is clear: in poor countries substantial transfers of income or wealth from the rich to the poor will be fiercely resisted and face great administrative costs and difficulties. In general, such transfers have taken place only after a revolution, which has its own economic costs. Therefore, the only way to increase the income of the poor majority rapidly and consistently is to enable the poor to earn more. This requires creating demand for their labour, their primary source of income. The more rapid and labour intensive the growth of the economy the more rapidly will jobs be created. Indeed, rapid growth seems to benefit the poor more than it does other groups.

Rapid growth also creates the wherewithal for government to set aside the reserves needed to prevent sharp declines in income. These are otherwise inevitable as the result of natural catastrophes and sharp increases in the prices of goods a country buys or large falls in the prices of goods it sells. In poor countries 15 to 40 per cent declines in income are hard to bear, especially if expectations have been raised by an earlier period of improvement in income.

Substantial disparities in income and wealth are inevitable in a capitalist system. They tend to be large, visible and hard to bear in poor countries. The continued poverty of the majority can lead to political tensions if the poor are constantly reminded of these disparities by the conspicuous consumption of the rich. Limiting visible consumption not only contributes to political stability but also encourages saving and investment. It is politically easier to achieve if the incomes of the middle and upper income groups are rising rapidly, as a corollary of rapid growth.

Even if per capita income is rising at 4 per cent or more a year, a high rate in terms of recent achievements, it will take a generation or two for most of the poor in poor countries to surmount absolute poverty. Therefore it matters a great deal whether they hope for improvement for themselves, or at least for their children. Rapid growth can furnish the resources to provide schooling for the children of the poor, a major element in hope for the future. Another element is assuring the poor majority that government is concerned with their lot. Avoiding rampant corruption is important for this reason as well as for efficiency. Reasonable pay for government employees can help limit corruption and is more readily financed in a growing economy.

The importance of an appropriate strategy

Rapid, labour intensive growth then is the key to poverty alleviation, to mitigating the effect of external shocks and to providing the resources to ease social tensions. Its achievement depends fundamentally on a set of government policies that do not aggravate market imperfections and distortions, but that compensate for them.

In an economy where labour is abundant and there is substantial unemployment and underemployment, and where capital and foreign exchange are scarce, *the worst strategy*:

- rations capital and foreign exchange but makes them cheap to those able to obtain them;
- makes labour expensive to employ in the organized, large-scale sector;
- tries to substitute government rules, controls, allocations and management for private incentives.

The net result is inefficiency, slow growth and windfall profits for those who can turn the control system to their advantage by influence, pressure or bribery. Worse, an increasing proportion of labour cannot find productive employment but ekes out an existence in low paid casual and sporadic labour. The result is increasing social and political tensions as large numbers see no hope for their families. Instead they see the benefits of the system going to those with the best connections, not to those who contribute the most. Rent and permit seekers become the winners, not producers or innovators.

A *better strategy* leaves the functioning of the economy to the market, to private enterprise, with a minimal role for government. In that system, if labour is abundant and capital and foreign exchange are scarce:

- labour will be cheap and therefore productively employed;

- capital and foreign exchange will be expensive and therefore business will use them carefully and work hard to generate more;
- private incentives will strongly encourage savings, hard work, risk taking and innovation.

The system will generate relatively rapid, labour intensive and efficient growth. Unskilled workers' wages will be uniformly low, but rise over time. Some inefficiency will be introduced in the system by inherent market imperfections and failures, and as the result of earlier government interventions that left a legacy of distortions that do not disappear overnight. As in all capitalist systems there will be considerable differences in income and wealth and consequent social and political tensions. Tensions will be exacerbated if much of the difference in economic success is not due to differences in ability or hard work but due to past or current discrimination, inheritance or past government favouritism.

The *best strategy* leaves the ownership and management of enterprises in private hands, and lets the market determine prices and distribution decisions, but government intervenes to:

- compensate for inherent imperfections in the market, such as the externalities (costs that are not internal to the firm) of breaking into the world market;
- compensate for distortions due to historical accident, past government interventions or institutional rigidities, such as unemployment due to labour costs that have been raised by past government intervention or inadequate foreign and domestic investment because the perceived risk is high;
- regulate or operate natural monopolies;
- reduce the tensions that arise if reforms cause extreme distress for some poor people or conspicuous consumption rises during periods of austerity and hardship for the majority, for instance by carrying out massive, labour intensive public works programmes financed by heavy taxes on conspicuous luxury consumption.

This strategy can achieve higher growth and greater labour intensity than one of complete *laissez faire*, or private enterprise, and therefore leads to more rapid poverty alleviation and the diffusion of social tensions. In addition, it would directly reduce such tensions and therefore the chances of backlash that would abort the reforms needed to achieve successful development in highly controlled economies.

The role of business

Since successful development depends primarily on the consistent implementation of an appropriate strategy, the most important role of the business community is in providing political support for such a strategy. This is easier said than done, since it requires that business act in concert, adopt a long-term perspective and support some policies whose direct immediate effect is unfavourable to business as a whole or to particular businesses.

There are then several obstacles to business playing the political role which could make the greatest difference in the success of development:

(1) The interest of the business community as a whole, the 'class interest' in Marxist terms, is in less government control of its actions, that is in reducing government intervention in the economy. But the interest of most firms is in retaining, and even expanding, government interventions that benefit that particular firm. Acting in its self-interest, each firm will press for expanding some interventions, although most will damage economic efficiency. While the owners and managers may favour less intervention as a principle, they will pursue this aim less passionately than interventions that benefit their firm directly and specifically. All of business, with each firm acting in its own interest, will then jointly be increasing government intervention. It is only by acting collectively, in their joint interest, that they will support reform even though some parts of the reform package damage a particular firm.

(2) Some reforms, some aspects of reduced government intervention, actually harm the interests of more businesses than they help, at least in the short term. For instance, in many economies more firms produce for the domestic than for the world market. Lower tariffs on balance then hurt the business community. It therefore will take a statesman-like, long-term view for business to support lower tariffs because they increase the efficiency of the economy and will, in the very long run, benefit a more efficient industry, oriented to the world market.

(3) To maintain support for reform will usually require taxing the wealthy, in particular taxing, and perhaps even restricting, some elements of their consumption. One reason would be to generate resources for measures to mitigate the negative effects of reforms on the most vulnerable groups. That, too, is something that the business community will normally resist. Yet it would be in its long-term interest to support it to avoid a serious backlash that could abort reforms that are favourable to business in the long term.

(4) With a declining share of the economy under government management and less control over the economy, there is greater need for government to strengthen monopoly control, regulate pollution, enforce public health and anti-fraud measures and strengthen consumer protection. Business would normally resist most of these measures. But if they are not taken it will strengthen opposition to

reform because its by-products include monopoly pricing by private firms, increased fraud and so on.

In short, to make its most important contribution to a successful development effort business will have to act collectively, in the long-term interest of the business community and the economy, and accept some measures it dislikes, in order to maintain widespread support for a more market-oriented strategy. This will not be easy, since the natural inclination of business firms, like that of most individuals and institutions, is to act in the individual firm's self-interest, to be concerned with the short term and to oppose government actions that it finds offensive.

There are additional actions that individual firms can take that will have a positive effect on development. Firms acting on their own can stress competence rather than connections, can provide training and a good working environment and so on. But if firms operate in a competitive situation, or if they just want to maximize their profits, what they can do in these respects is strictly limited by the environment of government policies in which they operate. If government rewards contacts, for instance, then firms too will need to be concerned with the influence their managers have, not with their abilities. The influence of business on government policies therefore is what really matters.

If the whole business community cannot or will not act to support reforms, because too many firms are concerned primarily with their own survival and short-term prosperity, then the reform effort will need to enlist part of business. Exporters and the more dynamic firms tend to be more supportive of reform. They get few benefits from the typical, highly protective system and can directly benefit from some reforms. Once the reform process is under way, if it is successful, it will expand and strengthen its own constituency. Nevertheless, until recently the business community has not played a major role in shaping and supporting reforms. It is an interesting question why that should be so.

Before one can answer that question, and discuss the role of business in greater detail, it is necessary to establish what makes for a successful development effort which business can support.

Elements of successful development

The economics of successful development

It is not difficult to define what constitutes clear and unequivocal 'success' in development: for poor countries it means an average growth rate in the national income of about 7 per cent or better, or in per capita income of 4 per cent or better for about two decades. At one time there was much esoteric argument among some specialists on whether 'economic growth', an increase in income, should be clearly distinguished from 'develop-ment', which requires in addition that the benefits of growth be widely distributed and be sustainable without extraordinary aid.

But by now the empirical evidence pretty clearly supports two propositions:

(1) Rapid growth can occur in a country for a decade or so with the benefits narrowly distributed and without the establishment of a sustainable process. Many countries achieved high growth rates in the 1970s, for instance, but grew slowly or declined in the 1980s. This group included countries in Africa (e.g. Ivory Coast, Gabon, Egypt, Cameroon), Latin America (e.g. Ecuador, Paraguay, Brazil) and Asia (Syria, Saudi Arabia). In most countries of unsustained, narrowly focused growth, the output increase was dependent on windfall gains from high prices for raw material exports (e.g. oil), or on heavy borrowing or massive foreign inflows, or all three.

If these, inevitably temporary, windfalls were poorly utilized, frittered away in conspicuous consumption or investment, the period of rapid growth was inevitably followed by a period of stagnation. Prices that had risen dropped again, loans became due, foreign investment and aid slowed, some unwise investments required continued costly subsidies and consumption levels, once ratcheted up, proved difficult to ratchet down again in response to tighter circumstances.

(2) But if rapid growth continues for two decades it usually means that the process is likely to be self-sustaining and continuous, with widespread benefits. Growth for such a long time almost inevitably creates rapidly rising demand for labour of all kinds, including unskilled labour. It therefore raises the labour income of unskilled workers, which means most of the poor. In addition, such persistent growth is rarely based on windfall gains only.

After two decades of growth a country usually has assured continued growth by:

- adopting policies which encourage entrepreneurial activity and savings;
- developing a set of institutions and habits which favour growth;
- making investments in human and physical capital which are productive and have competitive advantage in that country;
- learning to compete internationally; and
- by no means least, generating widespread support for the growth strategy which the country has adopted because of the widespread benefits which it has brought, thus allowing the strategy to continue.

All of these attributes yield continued returns to the economy when the windfall ends and/or generated the growth in the first place even in the absence of such a windfall.

Some of the countries that have been successful in those terms are well known: the five East Asian economies. Recently the list has often been limited to four countries. The achievement of the fifth, Japan, after the Second World War is equated with the recovery of Germany, and not considered an example of successful development. But Japan's per capita income in 1950 was only $250 (in 1964 dollars) even after recovery had progressed substantially. Its economic history in the 1950s and 1960s therefore had substantial elements of typical development, akin to South Korea a decade later.

For the last two decades three other South East Asian countries (Malaysia, Thailand, Indonesia) have joined Singapore in the successful group, as has, obviously, China. Two African countries are in the same group (Botswana and Mauritius, the latter because of low population growth) but none so far in South and Central America or West Asia (Oman has a high growth rate, but it is offset by an unusually high population growth rate).

Successful development, external shocks and flexible responses

All the success stories have had setbacks and will continue to have short periods of slow growth or even decline; all will eventually experience slowing growth – as everyone has discovered, even Japan must slow down at some point, no country can continue to grow indefinitely at 4 per cent per capita – and some may yet take a fatally wrong turn. Political disintegration or economic foolishness can derail the best established success story. But short of some radical change, these countries are set to continue increasing their per capita income at above average rates for the next decade, almost regardless of likely changes in the external environment.

The ability to absorb external shocks is a crucial difference between successful and less successful countries. Flexibility is built into a well-functioning market and into a well-functioning government policy machinery. Centrally planned or highly controlled economies, with their bureaucratic decision making process, find it much more difficult to deal with rapid change.

Flexibility in government policy, especially in shaping the macro-economic environment, is also important. It might be argued that the only policy government needs is to leave the market alone. But the most successful economies have had governments that adjusted quickly and anticipated major changes in the external environment.

The most obvious example is with respect to large windfall gains from temporary and substantial increases in income from a country's major export. The market is not good at anticipating and correcting in advance for the likelihood that income will decline equally sharply before too long.

Instead the market, reacting to current prices and incomes, tends to create the 'Dutch disease' problem.

The oil price increase of the 1970s is a good example. Oil exporting countries quickly developed an overvalued exchange rate. That made it unprofitable to produce goods that could be imported more cheaply and made it largely unprofitable to export anything but oil (and other natural resources). Industrial and agricultural production declined unless heavily subsidized, while importing, trade, finance and supplying government's needs flourished. Private firms responded to market incentives and became importers, traders and government contractors. No individual could change the incentive system; they could only respond to it. When oil revenues dropped sharply in 1982 governments and private individuals in many countries maintained their accustomed expenditures by borrowing, until this became prohibitively expensive. These countries then had to go through a very painful adjustment process, made all the more severe by being delayed.

Indonesia handled the problem better than most, because of more sensible government policies. It invested some of the windfall revenues in education and infrastructure. Other resources went to subsidize, sometimes via protection against imports, some of the productive activities that otherwise would not have been profitable at the exchange rate determined by the oil windfall. When the bonanza came to an end, Indonesia had a much stronger productive base in place than would have been the case without the various subsidies. Without doubt the system of subsidies was only fairly well designed and was distorted by political and personal factors. As a result, it was far less efficient than it could have been if designed by academic economists acting as platonic guardians. But it can be argued that the market, operating without subsidies, would have left the economy as ill-equipped to respond to the oil revenue decline as the Mexican, Venezuelan, Algerian and Nigerian economies proved to be. Moreover, once the dimensions of the problem became clear, the Indonesian government devalued the currency by 60 per cent and took a series of other steps that provided an effective, if hidden, subsidy to exporters. The environment was also made very attractive to foreign investors. The result has been an export boom which pulled Indonesia out of its slump much more quickly than was true for most other oil producers; it grew at nearly twice the rate of the average fuel exporter. Indonesia's relative success was almost wholly due to the greater flexibility of government policy, combined with broad scope for market action.

While flexibility, the ability to handle shocks, by markets and government policy are needed for success, it is highly likely that any economy which has grown rapidly for 20 years or more has learned some lessons on this score. Indeed, success teaches and reinforces successful behaviour. It also teaches that flexibility and risk-taking pay and that co-operation in large institutions can pay off for all who participate.

On the other hand, competitors often learnt the wrong lessons from failure; not to take the risk inherent in change, to think of the economy as a zero sum game and to act accordingly, to concentrate on manipulating government rather than responding to the market.

In short, the economies that have grown rapidly for a considerable time are generally the ones that are likely to perform well in the future and to remain success stories. A crucial element in success is to maintain political support for an economic strategy that works and support for an economic policy team in government that performs. That raises the question of the political economy of successful development.

The political economy of successful development

For a development strategy to be sustainable it must be perceived to be successful by the great majority of the population. This statement may not seem accurate, much less self-evident, to those who believe that politics in Less Developed Countries (LDCs) is essentially elite politics. Some of them argue that the great mass of illiterate people follow elite leadership. Therefore, as long as the elite is satisfied, government survival is assured.

A larger group consider authoritarian governments preferable for rapid early development, however regrettable they may declare this to be. An authoritarian government, they would argue, does not have to worry too much what the great majority thinks. It can therefore ruthlessly pursue the needs of growth, squeezing a maximum of resources out of the population to speed the process. In the longer term, the argument goes, everyone will be better off because the short-term well-being, and the political support of the majority could be ignored.

That argument has two flaws. The first, of course, is that there is no guarantee that an authoritarian government will use its undoubted powers to benefit the population, albeit in the long rather than the short run. Nor even that it will see development of the economy as an important objective, compared to, say, enriching itself in the short run, whatever the cost. There are as many examples of authoritarian governments that pursued short-term self-interest as there are of those that pursued the long-term interest, which would imply some attention to growth.

Second, there is some evidence that even authoritarian governments need to pay attention to the economic well-being of the majority of the population (Papanek, 1986). In the medium term of 3 to 7 years democracies vote out of office governments that do not improve economic well-being, decisively refuting the argument that the majority does not pursue self-interest but follows elite leadership. Under authoritarian governments, when elections are non-existent or rigged, people express the same dissatisfaction through riots or similar expressions of popular mood. A charismatic and populist leader who offers hope instead of bread or rice, can sometimes stave off the day of reckoning, but not for long. One ruthless enough may be able to suppress discontent for a long time, given modern methods in this field, but it remains a high risk gamble to assume that the economic welfare of the poor majority in poor countries can be ignored for any length of time.

Perceiving development as successful, or the 'index of perceived poverty'

Whether a government's economic strategy, its development effort, is perceived to be a success in turn depends on achieving, to at least some measure, the following four objectives:

(1) Increasing the income of the majority

Significant, longer-term increases in the income of the great majority of the population is an obvious essential for development to be considered a success. Conversely, long-term stagnation, or worse, decline, in the average income of the poorer majority of the population is the premier index of failure. However other-worldly their religious beliefs may be, there is plenty of very good evidence that most people in most societies are very much concerned with whether their income is going up or down, and have a very shrewd appreciation what its true direction is. They may not know the difference between nominal and real income, but they do know whether their purchasing power is increasing or not.

Experience has shown that raising the income of the poorer 30 to 60 per cent requires the creation of productive employment for the unemployed, the underemployed and the additions to the labour force among the unskilled, the great majority in poor countries. The alternative to increasing earned income is to increase income via transfer payments.

To take from the rich and give to the poor is not easy in wealthy countries. In poor countries it is immeasurably more difficult. There are too many poor and too few rich, and the poor are so miserably poor that the rich are panic struck at the thought of being forced to share.

Second, the administrative machinery is weak at taking from the rich. This is partly because administration in general is often weak and over-stretched by the needs of development. But more important is that the political leadership, the bureaucracy, the officer corps, the landed aristocracy and the business community all tend to be part of the same small elite, indeed often of the same family. It is asking a great deal that the political leadership should adopt policies to take income or wealth from family and friends, that the bureaucracy should administer such a programme and that the officer corps should support it, when it hits home or close to home. Finally, political pressures for transfers are weaker in what are often, at least *de facto*, one-party governments, than in systems where parties must bid for the votes of the poorer majority.

Third, for some of the same reasons the machinery finds it difficult to give to the poor. For both political and administrative reasons it is simply harder to redistribute a very small than a very large pie.

Beyond all these obstacles is the problem that poor countries need more powerful incentives to develop, and transfer payments usually weaken incentives. Strong incentives are needed because major shifts in behaviour are necessary. Petty traders, accustomed to quick turnover, need to be persuaded to become large-scale industrialists, investing for the long term. Farmers need to be persuaded to adopt modern technology, to take the risk of purchasing commercial inputs, to grow unknown and risky crops. People need to be persuaded to migrate long distances, perhaps to live among people who have different customs and languages, at least to move from the familiar village to the uncertain town. The needed economic incentives will be weakened if the successful lose some of their income to finance transfer payments.

Whatever the arguments for and against transfer payments, in practice massive transfers through the tax system, or of assets from rich to poor, have been rare, except as the result of revolution. Sri Lanka was a major exception until 1977. But transfers there were primarily from rich expatriate plantation owners to poor local voters and the political system was a rarity in Asia, Africa and Latin America: two parties that alternated in power as the result of voter dissatisfaction with those in power. Both parties therefore needed to appeal to the electorate and could do so at the cost of those who did not vote. But even in Sri Lanka the economic cost, and therefore the political cost, ultimately became too heavy and the massive transfers came to an end.

It is also not by accident that the Welfare State in Europe developed well after the Industrial Revolution. Given this experience, and the problems in the way of massive transfer payments, it is therefore quite reasonable to believe that in the currently poorer countries it is unlikely that much of the income of the poor will come as the result of massive transfer payments.

The only viable alternative to increasing the income of the poor majority then is for them to earn more. This they can do only if there is greater demand for the principal item they have for sale – their labour. Most of the poor have few, if any assets and they derive their income from work in agricultural, construction or other labour or in informal sector occupations as street peddlers, shoe shiners and so on, where most of their income is also derived from their labour.

How rapidly demand is created for this unskilled labour, in turn, depends essentially on how fast the economy is growing and how much labour is needed to support that growth, that is, how labour intensive the growth is. The more rapid and the more labour intensive the growth, the more rapid the increase in demand for labour and the more rapidly labour income will rise. Indeed, when the per capita income stagnates then the real wages of unskilled labour tend to decline and with them the income of the poor. On the other hand, for every percentage point increase in the growth rate the real wage of unskilled labour increases by more than 1 per cent on average (Papanek, 1989).

In effect, contrary to the argument by those who believe that 'small is beautiful' and that 'trickle down does not work', rapid growth is good for the poor. Indeed, there is good evidence that rapid growth benefits the poor more than it does the rest of the population. There is one exception, one caveat: the poor benefit only if growth is labour intensive, if it creates demand for their labour.

Probably the most important factor affecting political support for a development strategy and the government that carries it out is whether the strategy increases the income of the great majority of the population, many of whom are poor in poor countries. Increasing the income of the poor majority is crucially dependent on whether development generates demand for their labour. That in turn depends on how rapid and labour intensive the growth is.

(2) Mitigating and compensating for inevitable external shocks

Sooner or later the economy will suffer a sharp decline, however well managed it is. Droughts, floods or natural catastrophes will occur, the price of an important import (e.g. oil) will rise or the price of the most important export (e.g. gold or rice or cotton) will fall, or there will be a slump in the economy of the most important trading partners, resulting in a drastic loss in markets. The consequence can be a sharp decline in income for very large groups in the population. If these are not mitigated or counteracted those affected will usually blame the economic policies of the government rather than the external cause, with serious consequences for popular support of the government and its economic strategy.

Even if incomes have been rising quite rapidly on average over a 10-year period, a 2 to 3 year short-term setback to people's economic well-being can cause great anger. A decline in income of 20 to 40 per cent in the course of 1 to 2 years can be devastating to a poor family. It can be especially difficult to accept when expectations and commitments have been raised by a previous period of improving incomes. It is only natural that after a 4 to 5-year period of prosperity the expectation is that incomes and opportunities will continue to increase. Moreover, even poor people will make commitments on the basis of such expectations. Children will be enrolled in school, with a continuing commitment to pay school fees and to buy books. A bicycle may have been bought and money borrowed to pay for it. Squatters may have moved from free areas to better housing where a rent is due, and so on.

If income then suddenly declines sharply instead of continuing to rise as expected, the disappointment and anger can be all the stronger, producing the strongest political reaction. Conversely, the favourable political reaction will be especially strong if income rises after a period of stagnation. Expectations and commitments will be low and people will be pleasantly surprised by the unexpected improvement in their economic well-being. It is, therefore, the successful government with the effective strategy, or one that for other reasons has aroused the highest expectations, that needs to be most concerned with unexpected short-term setbacks to the economy. Yet such setbacks are inevitable.

A comprehensive strategy therefore anticipates the inevitability of external shocks to the economy and adopts policies before any occur that will mitigate the effect of the shocks. This is a function that only government can perform. There have been three major steps that governments have taken to reduce the impact of external shocks on the poor majority.

The most important measure has been a reserve stock of staple foods to prevent sharp temporary increases in the prices of foods consumed by poorer people. Such increases are otherwise inevitable as a result of bad harvests, either in the country or in the exporting countries if it is an importer. This is an obvious measure, but it is not simple to manage. There is always the risk that the reserve stocks will be used not to even out temporary fluctuations but to try to counteract longer-term changes. Farmers will exert pressure for government to buy more than needed for stabilization purposes in order to increase the prices they receive. If there are organized consumers their interest will be in government selling more than prudent during periods of rising prices. The most effective stabilization agencies therefore have had some degree of autonomy and some clear guidelines on when to sell and when to buy.

To deal with the other major source of external shocks, arising in the world market, the best insurance is an adequate reserve of foreign exchange. This again is difficult to manage. When a country benefits from favourable export prices there is the strong temptation to use the resulting income to take care of the many urgent and important needs that usually exist. It is politically difficult, but nevertheless important, for government to use budgetary resources (or to work through the central bank) to set aside some of the windfall gains, to be used to maintain needed imports when the inevitable downturn in foreign exchange earning or transfers occurs.

Some governments have also put a guaranteed floor under the price received by farmers for some major crops. Without such a guarantee many smallholders are unable or unwilling to take the risk:

- to purchase on credit commercial inputs, such as fertilizer, in adequate amounts because they are afraid that the price they receive for their output may fall so much that they cannot pay off their loans, still feed their families and retain their land;
- to shift from the production of lower value food crops to the production of higher cash crops, because of their fear that the price of food could rise sufficiently, or of the cash crop fall sufficiently, to make it impossible for them to buy the food they need and retain their land.

Smallholders are very risk averse. Even if it pays in an average year to buy commercial inputs, or to shift to higher value cash crops, they will be reluctant to do so if they risk losing their land in the one year out of 10 which is far below average. If it is in the interest of society that they take the risk, because the result will be higher income and lower food prices for the country, then it can be very much worthwhile to insure farmers against excessive risk by putting a floor under some major crop prices.

In combination, these three social insurance policies can dampen the extreme fluctuations in prices that would otherwise take place in the short run. Since the poor suffer especially from short-run inflation this can reduce the sharp short-term setbacks to the purchasing power, or the real income, of the majority which has such strong destabilizing effects.

(3) Limiting the conspicuous consumption of the rich

The gap between rich and poor is particularly apt to cause social and political problems in poor countries, where poverty is stark and the gap tends to be large. The tensions are exacerbated further if rich and poor are primarily from different ethnic groups and if mobility from one to the other is limited.

Differences in income usually do not matter, however, because income is not visible, but differences in consumption can be quite evident, particularly if the rich engage in conspicuous consumption (e.g. luxurious automobiles or houses, conspicuous partics, weddings and other celebrations). These can generate anger and envy. The political consequences will be especially great if a shift to a market economy eliminates restrictions on the import of luxury goods. In some countries the first effects of liberalization were an obvious increase in conspicuous consumption and the simultaneous threat of unemployment for many workers in public enterprises. That is a sure prescription for political trouble. Limits on conspicuous consumption can then contribute to social peace, political stability and continued support for a market-oriented development strategy.

In addition, limits on conspicuous consumption generally promote savings and investment. They can encourage the rich to compete to see who can establish the biggest business empire rather than who builds the biggest house or drives the biggest car. If consumption is difficult and costly because it is heavily taxed or otherwise restricted, then saving and investing one's income will generally be more attractive. Savings rates of 50 per cent or more out of industrial profits have been achieved under these circumstances (Papanek, 1967).

(4) Giving people hope

Almost regardless of the speed and pattern of economic development it takes 20 to 40 years before a great majority of poor people in poor countries begin to move out of dire poverty. Their attitude towards a government and its economic strategy then can be affected a great deal by whether it gives them hope that they, and even more important, their children, will be better off in the future.

A few illustrative numbers will make this clear. If the economy grows at 6.5 per cent a year, which is double the average for low and middle income countries in the 1980s, and population grows at a typical 2.0 per cent so that per capita income grows at 4.5 per cent per year, then it will take over 15 years for income per person to double. The poorest 40 per cent of the population typically have only 8 to 25 per cent of total income. In poor countries it would then take them 30 years or so, or one generation, to go from a very poor $130 per person per year to a still poor $500. In any 2 to 3 year period the improvement in their well-being is therefore modest. Whether the government gives people hope for the future can therefore matter in determining their evaluation of the success of the economic strategy.

One factor that generates hope for the future is the steady and visible improvement in income which has already been discussed in terms of its effect in creating better living conditions. It not only changes current well-being but also creates hope for the future. Two other factors which significantly affect hope are:

- whether children in the family have access to education, universally seen as the principal passport to a better life, and to reasonable medical care so that they are likely to survive to adulthood;
- whether government is seen to care about the well-being of the majority of the population or is seen as indifferent and concerned only with the elite.

One factor in whether government is perceived as caring is the nature and pervasiveness of corruption. Clearly a government that can be bought is more responsive to the rich and powerful than to the poor. It is sometimes argued that corruption does not matter much to the great majority. They are either untouched by it or they expect and accept it as one of the perquisites of power and family. Within relatively narrow limits both may indeed be true. If the economy, and the lot of the majority, is improving and if corruption mainly takes the form of money changing hands at the highest level of government without seriously affecting the functioning of the economy, then concern with corruption may be limited to small groups within the elite. But there is plenty of evidence by now – from the defeat of the Kuomintang government in China, to the bitterness against Marcos and the riots in Zaire – that widespread corruption creates powerful hostility to the government. Corruption may start at the top and initially affect only which of two equally qualified contenders is given the nod; but it tends to spread until virtually everyone is affected in their daily lives.

Another factor in how government is perceived is the image the leadership projects. If many people are suffering, for instance because of temporary exogenous shocks, while government claims that all is well, then the conclusion that people can justifiably reach is that the government in power is either ignorant of, or indifferent to, their lot. On the other hand, a leader can show concern by emphasizing that he knows people are suffering, that he is determined to improve their situation and by announcing populist measures. The measures may be largely cosmetic and may have long-term costs for the poor, but in the short term they can generate a good deal of support.

Evidence on the political economy of economic strategy

That these four factors matter, that they affect the actions of people outside the elite, is by no means clearly established, but it is more than a purely theoretical hypothesis. In the case of five Asian countries one can tell stories in which negative changes in the four factors were followed, in most cases, by strong expressions of discontent. In the two of these five countries (India and Sri Lanka) with regular and open elections the government party was defeated when the four factors turned negative. In the three countries where elections as an outlet for discontent were not usually available, riots and other widespread disturbances took place. Conversely, when the four factors were positive, governments won elections or enjoyed a calm political situation.

The statistical relationship was a fairly strong one, with the relationship generally as hypothesized (see Papanek, 1986 for tables covering Bangladesh, India, Indonesia and Pakistan). But in about one-quarter of the cases the relationship between changes in the four factors (called 'the index of perceived poverty') and political events was ambiguous or the opposite of the hypothesis. An improvement in the four measures of economic well-being was followed by electoral defeat or riots and vice versa. That is as one would expect. It would be surprising indeed if the changes in these four measures perfectly predicted political events. Much more likely is that these indices imperfectly measure economic changes, that economic changes in turn had some influence on political events but that other factors, mostly in the political realm and including religious or ethnic conflict, political organization or leadership, were decisive in many political developments.

Thus, there is some evidence that for an economic strategy to be regarded as successful and to retain widespread support it needs to:

- Raise the income of the majority of the population, as one might expect. This in turn requires rapid, labour intensive growth.
- Mitigate inevitable short-term setbacks due to exogenous factors. Only government can create the reserves needed to prevent sharp declines in income for several years as the result of natural catastrophes and sharp changes in world prices, which are especially hard to bear once expectations have been raised.
- Limit conspicuous consumption of the rich. Great disparities in income and wealth are inevitable in a capitalist system. The continued poverty of the majority can lead to political tensions if the poor are constantly reminded of these disparities by the conspicuous consumption of the rich. Limiting visible consumption not only contributes to political stability but also encourages saving and investment.
- Give hope to people who will inevitably remain poor for at least a generation by providing opportunities for schooling for their children and by assuring them that government is concerned with their lot. Limiting corruption is important for this reason as well as for efficiency.

The central role of growth in poverty alleviation and political support

There is another conclusion that follows this discussion: the centrality of growth. To some degree the development economics fraternity has come full circle in recognizing the importance of economic growth to economic well-being and to the amelioration of socio-political problems. For more than a decade the emphasis on growth was decried because it was argued that worsening income distribution went so far as to suggest that the poor typically were absolutely worse off in the early stages of development. An emphasis on growth was equated with unjustified faith in 'trickle down', the presumed belief that the poor would ultimately benefit from growth, but that it might take a long time before the benefits reached them.

As the result of doubts that growth quickly alleviated poverty the emphasis shifted to 'growth with distribution' or to 'satisfying basic needs'. The latter argued for a welfare state approach even in the early stages of development. 'Dependency' theorists went further still, arguing that only a fundamental, really revolutionary, redistribution of assets would achieve a substantial improvement in the well-being of the poor majority.

Developments during the last decade have partly discredited these alternative approaches. Most important is the accumulating evidence that poverty generally declined in countries where per capita income was growing rapidly, while the number of poor increased during periods of stagnation or decline in per capita income. However, there were exceptions (see World Bank, 1990).

Second, the alternative approaches, emphasizing direct attacks on poverty and including some redistributive elements, proved to have severe limits. Due to the combination of political resistance and administrative difficulties, already discussed, the amounts that could be transferred were modest.

Third, even limited redistribution was difficult unless the income of the rich grew rapidly even after redistribution. That meant that the economy as a whole needed to grow quite rapidly.

In short, rapid growth therefore not only reduced poverty directly, it also served to make redistributive measures politically feasible. With a rapidly growing economy, a labour intensive pattern of growth and some minor redistributive measures poverty could decline quite quickly, as it did in Indonesia from 1970 to 1987 (World Bank, 1990). Rapid growth also provided the resources needed for the economic prerequisites for continued political support. It facilitated government financing of the reserves needed to mitigate the effects of external shocks; it increased the plausibility of leadership statements designed to provide hope; and it made it easier for the rich to accept some limits on their conspicuous consumption because their income was rising and the restrictions on consumption were unlikely to last long.

The role of government and market in successful development

There is by now near universal agreement that successful development, which achieves both a high rate of growth and rapid poverty alleviation, depends above all on a government strategy which does not severely distort market incentives and which then allows market incentives to determine the behaviour of individual firms. Development clearly is a complex process, influenced by many factors. It matters whether a society is thrifty or not, whether the political system is reasonably stable, whether money is approved or frowned upon, whether the prices of major exports are rising or falling, whether the business community is experienced, how good the educational system is, how much foreign capital is flowing in, whether the population/resources ratio is a favourable one or not, how rapidly population is growing and so on. But handicaps can be overcome or advantages squandered by an appropriate or distorting set of government policies (see for instance Papanek, 1967, 1988). The strategy adopted is decisive.

There is widespread agreement that the worst performance with respect to economic growth and in the alleviation of poverty has been registered in countries where governments' policy has worsened inherent market imperfections, created massive distortions in prices and incentives, and where government has operated and managed a large proportion of the individual enterprises in the economy. A far better performance, both with respect to growth and poverty alleviation, then has resulted in economies where government has played a minimal role in the economy and has let the market and private enterprise operate with little intervention.

But there remain some disagreements on the extent to which government should intervene in positive ways to achieve an even better performance. The disagreement centres on four issues.

The extent of government management or control

Some activities, primarily the provision of infrastructure and social services, tend to be natural monopolies: the provision of public health, of roads, railways and communications. There is general agreement that such natural monopolies need either to be operated by government or government needs to exercise some control over their prices. The disagreement is with respect to whether ownership/operation or control is more desirable.

This is often an empirical and pragmatic question, with the best solution depending on circumstances. In any case, the answer on this issue is not generally considered crucial in determining whether development is successful or not.

'Picking winners' – the role of industrial policy

The most controversial issue is with respect to 'industrial policy', the extent to which government is better able than private enterprise to determine in which industries massive investment is in the long-run interest of a country. An even more important role for government then is to assure that investment actually takes place in those industries. The advocates of industrial policy sometimes believe that the investment should be undertaken by public enterprises. Others urge that government should subsidize private investment in these sectors, usually through protection of the initial investment against competition from imports, sometimes by targeted credit and other subsidies.

The proponents of industrial policy point to the success of Japan, South Korea, Taiwan and, to a lesser extent, some countries in South East Asia in support of their position. The opponents point to two dangers in this approach:

(1) that governments can make mistakes in picking winners, indeed are more likely to make mistakes since they are not risking their own money; and
(2) that they may persist in mistaken policies for much longer than private firms would, since the political costs of admitting error may be greater than those of backing their gamble with further resources.

The opponents sometimes cite the same countries in support of their argument. The decision of South Korea to invest in energy intensive industries just ahead of the oil price increases of the 1970s is a favourite example.

The advocates have recently made some headway by citing achievements of the East Asian governments (including Japan and China) in promoting industries that became successful exporters. But in citing these examples, it is necessary to distinguish the relative importance of the government's role in picking particular industries and its role in compensating for market imperfections, the next point of disagreement.

Compensating for market imperfections

Even the most dedicated advocates of private enterprise and the market recognize that there are some market imperfections. One that is of substantial importance is the existence of externalities: costs imposed by one economic actor on another, or benefits that similarly accrue to others than those who generate them. A standard example, of increasing importance recently, is the pollution created by one firm that raises the costs of downwind or downstream firms and consumers.

Less widely recognized as an externality is the cost of breaking into the world market for manufactured goods. The ability to sell products where quality is important and difficult to measure depends very much on reputation. That in turn is substantially affected by the location of the firm.

In the early 1950s Japanese firms had the reputation of producing cheap but shoddy goods and every exporter from Japan had to overcome that reputation. In the 1980s Japanese firms benefited from the general reputation of producing high quality. The change in reputation was achieved at considerable cost by exporters that painfully established a good reputation in the face of assumptions to the contrary. Moreover, pioneer exporters had to devote considerable resources to learn about the requirements of different foreign markets, to explore marketing channels, to find the markets where they could compete and to establish contact with reliable buyers. Japanese latecomers to exporting in general and with respect of particular commodities could obtain this information at much less cost. Therefore Japanese exporters of industrial goods initially faced substantial negative externalities; subsequently they benefited from positive ones.

Only society as a whole, acting through government, can compensate for the costs of economy-wide negative externalities and develop positive externalities. This is true as well for other market imperfections. For instance, in the case of pioneer manufactured exports, government can provide a general subsidy to all firms who break into the world market with commodities that need to establish a reputation for quality. That subsidy would compensate pioneer exporters for special costs they incur simply because they are located in a country that has not historically exported such manufactures.

The governments of most East Asian countries have extensively intervened in the economy to compensate for market imperfections. Initially they protected infant industries to compensate them for the cost of learning by doing and for the cost of organized training that pioneer industries had to incur. A major element in their success were the policies which very quickly made exporting profitable, despite the additional costs incurred by pioneer exporters: a favourable exchange rate, subsidized credits, various other special government concessions, import privileges or drawback schemes, etc. These governments also invested heavily in social and physical infrastructure, including education, which combine the characteristics of natural monopolies and major externalities.

In short, it can be argued that their success, and that of some South East Asian countries, was far less due to the ability of government to pick industrial winners than to its ability to establish policies which compensated all firms for the cost of market imperfections. At the same time firms were systematically exposed to competitive pressures, the only effective guarantee for increasing efficiency and lower costs.

Achieving social objectives

It is generally recognized that while the market is efficient in achieving economic objectives it is not necessarily ideal in reaching social goals. Rapid labour intensive growth is indeed favourable for poverty alleviation, but the speed of poverty alleviation may be inadequate in terms of the social or political aims of a society. Government then needs to intervene to transfer income or assets to the poor or to provide a minimum level of necessities to them.

How far should government intervene?

While there is consensus that government intervention in these four aspects of the economy *can* improve the functioning of both economy and society, there is a great deal of controversy whether it in fact *will* improve or worsen the situation. The sceptics believe that government intervention as a whole must be severely limited and that it should not take place at all with respect to one or more of the aspects listed. Because government intervention is inevitably shaped by political considerations, they believe that it will tend to extend way beyond what is desirable and will worsen distortions and imperfections, not compensate for them.

They have a great deal of evidence on their side. There are many examples, in South Asia, Latin American and Africa (and of course in the Communist countries and in places like Burma), of government over-reaching, of aggravating distortions and imperfections and of slowing growth and poverty alleviation. There are few examples, primarily in East Asia, of government intervention that had predominantly favourable results. But as a result of the recognition of this experience there has been overcorrection in some countries, with too much faith and reliance in the market. That is particularly dangerous in an economy where distortions are great as a result of excessive government intervention in the past. A quick leap to reliance on the market can then result in a sharp economic decline.

Based on the evidence, it is justifiable to conclude that the best performance has been registered by economies where government has intervened substantially, to compensate for existing distortions and market imperfections, whether they have resulted from past government interventions or from inherent weaknesses of the market. How much government intervention and in what form is desirable undoubtedly varies from country to country and over time. It is certainly affected by the strength and honesty of government, both the political leadership and the civil service, as well as by the stage of development. When appropriate policies and programmes are easily discerned and simple to execute, then government can be more effective than when the economy and the environment in which it operates are both highly complex and rapidly changing. The market can respond more quickly and effectively in the latter situation, despite its imperfections.

The second point is that while there are some disagreements about the desirable limits to government's role, there is a remarkable intellectual consensus, probably for the first time in this century, on the desirability of a relatively limited role for government and a prominent role for market forces. There is now surprisingly widespread agreement with what had always been the dominant business view, that the great majority of enterprises should be privately owned and managed, operating in response to the profit motive in a market where prices are set by market forces. Even the resurgent Communist parties that have gained power in some of the countries of Eastern Europe and the former Soviet Union claim to be in favour of a market system. The only widely recognized exceptions to private ownership and the use of market incentives for enterprises are those that are natural monopolies or where external costs or benefits are very large.

Obstacles to successful, market-based development

This consensus on a dominant role for private enterprise and the market in firm operation and decision making, price setting and commodity flows means that half the battle to achieve rapid growth is won before it is joined. The widespread agreement on the economic system appropriate for success in growth and poverty alleviation contrasts with the fierce ideological battles about the most effective system that have been waged over much of the last century. But the economic millennium has not arrived, and there remain serious obstacles to the adoption of an effective strategy for rapid growth and poverty alleviation.

'Great Leap Forward' or 'all deliberate speed'

While there is agreement on the nature of an effective system, there is genuine and serious disagreement on how to get there from the current situation for many countries, with much of the economy owned and operated by public enterprises and even more of the economy controlled in some detail by government. These disagreements have slowed and in some cases reversed reforms.

Until recently the dominant view on the best path to follow might be called 'The Great Leap Forward'. There were various arguments for moving as quickly as possible to a market system:

(1) Gradual progress allowed the opposition time to mobilize its forces and to abort the reforms before they became irreversible.
(2) There are good theoretical reasons for believing that removing only some distortions would not necessarily improve the functioning of the economy, as long as other distortions remained. The only sure road to success was to remove all major distortions.
(3) There were undoubtedly costs to the adjustment process, and radical solutions shortened the period of suffering, while a gradual process only prolonged the agony.
(4) Both the external reform forces and the supporting international community exerted maximum influence when the failures of the old control system were most evident and when a large package of aid was on offer. Once aid had begun to flow and, together with the first fruits of reform, had ameliorated the situation the pressure for reform would fade and crucial further steps might never be taken.

There have been second thoughts about this radical strategy of instant reform, especially among policy makers. However, some of the economists who originally argued (by false analogy to my mind) that 'you cannot leap a chasm in two bounds' remain persuaded of the superiority of that strategy. It has become apparent that the radical, all at once, changes can mobilize very fierce opposition. That opposition has been very effective in a number of countries, where it has helped bring to power governments that have promised to slow reform. Indeed, the obvious costs of instant reform have, in a few cases, even helped elect governments which represent the old Communist Party under a new name. That people should pine for the bad old Communist days is, in part, a reflection of the costs of a rapid shift from a controlled to a market-oriented system.

The other arguments in favour of drastic, quick reforms also seem less persuasive now, given the apparently greater relative success of countries pursuing more gradual change. The 'Great Leap' countries include the former Soviet Union, some of the East European countries and such countries as Chile. More gradual reforms were carried out in China, Mexico and a few East European countries recently and earlier in most of the East Asian and South East Asian success stories. Not all gradual reforms are successful, nor do all radical reforms generate a more serious backlash, but at least there are serious doubts about the superiority of the radical path as a result of both recent and earlier experience.

The opposition of vested interests

However attractive a move to the market may be to the business community as a general proposition, every reform imposes costs on some group, and usually a powerful group. If a reform had only benefits and no serious costs, it would undoubtedly have been carried out long ago. It is rare that costless reforms are not implemented only because those framing policy are ignorant about their possible benefits. Decision makers may not have quantified the economic costs and benefits of a policy, but they usually are quite aware of the benefits which economists anticipate and they are very much aware of likely political costs.

Competition is considered desirable, but not if it reduces the profitability of one's own enterprise. In that case it is resisted by the affected owners, managers and workers. Privatization is often fiercely opposed by the workers of the enterprise if the plant is overstaffed and workers fear the loss of their jobs. Managers welcome privatization if it gives them control over government assets at little cost, but not if there is the danger that new owners will look for more competent management (or, less nobly, prefer family members to be in charge, even if less competent). Consumers oppose reduced subsidies. Virtually every change will generate opposition from those negatively affected, or those who think they might be.

Usually there are clear, concentrated, immediate and certain costs to the groups which lose from reforms. The benefits tend to be diffuse, uncertain and delayed. Opposition is therefore stronger and better organized than support. That has been a key problem in carrying out specific reforms, even when there is consensus on the desirability of a reform strategy.

Short-term inequities and income losses

In addition to resistance from better-off and elite groups who lose special benefits and unearned rents as the result of reform, there are often costs for the poor as well in the short term. There may also be a rise in income disparities. As a result, groups concerned with poverty alleviation and inequality may oppose reforms even if their own self-interest is not affected.

If structural reforms are carried out at the same time as a stabilization effort then these problems may be especially severe. The standard stabilization programme depresses demand in order to deal with inflation, balance of payments problems and budget deficits. The result is a decline in income, which can have especially severe consequences for the poor whose income is already low.

As already noted, one result may be political tensions, electoral defeat or riots. Governments afraid of these consequences will often avoid carrying out reforms. If they do carry them out, they may pay for this by losing power and their successors will draw the lesson of slowing or reversing reforms.

The sequencing of successful reforms

Opposition can be reduced if the sequencing of reforms produces immediate benefits in higher growth. In that case the negative impact can be limited, or even be turned into immediate benefits, for both elite groups that will lose some of the rent they previously gained from protection and the poor who may lose some subsidies.

Which reforms can produce immediate gains depends very much on the circumstances of particular countries, but the experience of countries that were successful in this respect provides some guidelines. Expansionary reform took place in Indonesia, South Korea, Taiwan and China among others. More limited reforms that yielded quick benefits took place in South Asia in the 1960s (Pakistan, Bangladesh) and late 1970s (Sri Lanka). Most carried out three measures that could yield immediate benefits.

(1) *Make exports more profitable and thereby increase export production.* Many of the countries had some idle capacity for increased production that could not be used because there was no market for the output at current costs and prices or because the needed imported inputs were

not available. By increasing the profitability of exports that idle capacity was put to work, creating jobs and income. The problem of inadequate demand was solved by opening up the world market. Imported inputs could be made available because the added exports provided the needed foreign exchange to buy them. In addition, exporters were usually exempted from various restrictions on imports.

(2) *Increase agricultural production by reducing distortions affecting that sector.* In economies where family farms operate much of agricultural land (even if the family does not always own it) there is usually underutilized labour available to increase production. In addition, there is scope for increasing output by using more commercial inputs or using them more efficiently. Output can then be quickly increased if the incentive system facing cultivators is made economically more rational. That might include ending government purchase of output below market prices; monopoly distribution of inputs; and distorted relative prices of different crops.

(3) *Increase the efficiency of public sector enterprises.* For some enterprises this might involve privatization. It was typical of the successful countries that privatization was a relatively slow process: but public enterprises are usually operated so inefficiently that substantial gains are possible in the course of the first year by improving their functioning even while they remain in public hands.

There were several factors which affected the ability of some of the successful countries to sequence and structure the reforms to yield net benefits in the short term:

- Structural reforms did not have to be carried out at the same time as a drastic adjustment programme. Unlike other countries, they had not been consuming substantially more than they produced, exhausting their foreign exchange reserves and/or borrowing to finance the difference. A sharp and inevitably painful downward adjustment in consumption could therefore be avoided. If such an adjustment happens at the same time as structural reform, then reforms will usually be blamed for the hardship that is really caused by the profligate ways adopted earlier (perhaps by a different government). The successful countries generally needed only a minor stabilization programme which did not involve a radical reversal from rising to sharply declining consumption.
- Several benefited from substantial aid flows in the early stages of reform.
- Several adopted a deliberate programme to mitigate any negative effects for the most vulnerable groups while maintaining austerity in consumption.
- The adjustment process was well managed. The analytical work

underlying the reforms had been relatively well done and the political system was one which allowed the government considerable room for manoeuvre.

Once the first reforms produced quick benefits it was obviously a good deal easier to maintain the momentum of reform than if the immediate consequences had been substantial costs for much of the population. In other countries where the costs were immediate some governments were able to continue reform only by suppressing dissatisfaction until the benefits of reform became evident, which can take 3 to 6 years. In still others there has been a backlash against reforms which resulted in their abandonment. Governments carrying out reform programmes often hope that they will be able to survive the period when the reforms seem to have mostly costs because the pain will be of short enough duration, or that foreign resources will mitigate it sufficiently, or that people will be sufficiently persuaded of the desirability of reform to tolerate the temporary costs. Clearly far better though is a reform programme that yields net benefits in the short-term.

The political economy of reform then involves a careful sequencing of policy changes. Early reforms need to be designed to bring relatively quick and visible gains, while limiting the damage and the perceived threat to enterprises that will lose as a result of greater reliance on the market. Early measures usually should include stronger incentives to exporters and loosening control over those moving into the export market. Import liberalization also begins with the inputs needed by exporters. Only when exports have begun to expand significantly, and to provide employment and profits, are imports liberalized that will strongly compete with firms that have produced for the domestic market shielded by strong protection.

It is equally important during the early stages not to deregulate consumption ahead of the deregulation of production. If luxury consumption has been tightly controlled for years and is suddenly freed from most restrictions, one of the first consequences of reform will be the appearance on the streets of luxury automobiles not seen for years and the proliferation of other consumer durables. At the same time, lower and middle-income groups can be hit by higher prices as a result of decontrol and reduced subsidies and by job losses as their employers are unable to compete with cheaper imports. The combination of rising conspicuous consumption and hardship for large groups is a sure prescription for social unrest and political trouble.

Instead, among the early results of reforms should be the creation of new jobs in export industries and, in some countries, in agriculture; lower prices as a result of increased competition in trade and as cheaper mass consumption goods are imported; and some increase in employment and income as a result of greater domestic demand stemming from growing exports and agricultural production, plus more foreign private investment and foreign aid and the greater availability of cheaper imported inputs into industry.

Reform can quickly generate its own momentum if it is seen to result in some increase in employment and income, with no increase in luxurious living by the rich. A constituency will have been created for the next steps in reform which will involve more substantial costs. Besides, these costs are easier to absorb in a swiftly growing economy. Once there has been widespread improvement as the result of reform then increased consumption by the rich is easier to tolerate.

The role of business

The central issue: business influence on economic strategy

The argument so far then is that successful development depends fundamentally on the environment and incentives created by government policy. Therefore, as summarized earlier, the major contribution which the business community can make to economic success would be to support an appropiate set of government policies. No doubt in a market system there is also an important role for business, and especially for entrepreneurs, in management and innovation with respect to individual enterprises. But government policy critically influences even these aspects of business's role. Only if the policy-determined incentive structure is an appropriate one can business perform its function so that Adam Smith's 'invisible hand' assures that the pursuit of self-interest by each individual also effectively achieves benefits for society as whole. If the incentive structure is sufficiently distorted it is perfectly possible that the more effectively business pursues its self-interest the more damage it does to the economy as a whole.

If the most effective way of making a large profit is to get a government permit that generates large rents, then the more successful the individual is in using bribery or pressure to obtain such permits the more resources are squandered and the more impoverished others are. For instance, where import licences for luxury consumer goods are scarce, whoever extracts one from the government machinery can make lots of money without adding anything to national income. Similarly, where exports of oil are licensed, with oil sold on the world market for $1 and purchased domestically at a controlled price of $0.10, the more is exported the greater the profits for business holding export licences but the greater the national resources that are wasted.

These are both cases where it might be constructive for government to get out of the way and to let the market function. But if unlimited imports of luxury goods cause counterproductive tensions, then substituting heavy excise taxes for quantitative restrictions would be even more constructive. Similarly, it may not be possible to raise the domestic price of oil to the world price in one step without serious disruption of the economy, but export duties can substitute for export licences with major benefits to the economy.

The point of these examples is to stress again the importance that government policy plays in determining how efficiently private business functions in generating income and growth. It follows that the policies and strategies which individual enterprises pursue are often less important to the speed and nature of growth than the role of business as a group in influencing government policy. Before returning to this theme it is worth examining what individual business enterprises and business groups can do to speed development.

Direct actions by business enterprises and groups

Among the direct functions of business emphasized as important in economic development the following are usually mentioned:

- training of labour, technical and professional staffs;
- developing a modern business culture which rewards competence in managers and entrepreneurs;
- transferring technology internationally and within the country from one enterprise to another;
- subcontracting by larger enterprises to smaller ones;
- accumulating investment capital;
- establishing constructive labour relations.

These are all clearly important functions, but even their performance is substantially determined by relevant government policies.

Training of workers, technicians and professionals

Training of labour is particularly important in an economy where much of the population has not been part of the modern commercial sector. Training then even includes instilling the importance of punctuality and regularity of attendance, the significance of maintaining machinery and how to perform small-scale repair. Mid-level managers, engineers and technicians also must obtain much of their training on the job, especially in societies where the educational system is highly academic and abstract.

The appropriate role of government in the training process is both crucial and limited. On the one hand there is ample evidence by now that government vocational training programmes are rarely effective. The public educational system is crucial in providing basic and general education:

literacy, numeracy, knowledge of how the world functions and so on. It can also train students in general vocational and technical skills and in the professions. But specific applied skills are usually best learned on the job, or in some combination of formal schooling and on the job training.

Yet how much training business provides is greatly influenced by government policy. For any business enterprise only a very limited amount of training is profitable, far less than is desirable for the economy as a whole. That is because there are large externalities to a great deal of training, benefits that cannot be fully captured by the enterprise incurring the cost. Once an enterprise has incurred the cost of both organized training and the cost of errors as workers, technicians, engineers and managers learn on the job, another enterprise can reap many of the benefits by hiring the trained employees away at a slightly higher salary. Unless the social system assures a lifetime commitment of employer and employee to each other, the enterprise has to take account of the likelihood that it will not gain the full benefits from the training costs it incurs. Worse, its competitors will actually be part beneficiaries and will therefore be better placed to outcompete the firm that has done the training.

As on many other tasks, private business is best able to provide the practical, specific and on the job training which is needed; but government needs to create the incentive structure so that the amount and nature of training which is provided is what the economy and society need. That means any firm which pioneers a particular form of training needs to be subsidized to reflect the external benefits it creates for other firms which find a trained and experienced labour force available without the need to incur training costs.

Subsidies can be provided in various ways:

(1) The training can be provided by a government enterprise that expects to have its competent and experienced labour force hired away shortly after the training process is completed (or which is privatized after most of the training costs are incurred). Apparently by happenstance a number of public enterprises in Latin America performed this function. Government pioneered the metal and metal working industries and incurred the heavy costs of training machine operators, including the substantial costs of producing defective parts. A private industry then developed which hired away the managers, skilled workers and technicians. One problem with that approach is that the public firm may apply pressure to prevent private competition from developing. Another is that workers may also learn bad habits in firms that can ignore profitability.

(2) Government can mandate industry-wide training programmes. A small fee can be imposed on the output of all firms in an industry, with the proceeds used to subsidize training and apprenticeship programmes in

any firm in that industry. The programme can be administered by the industry concerned, with government only providing the legal basis for mandatory fee collection. Subsidized training by industry, financed by an industry levy, seems to have worked well in some South American countries.

(3) Government can use tax revenue to subsidize training and apprenticeship programmes by individual firms.

All subsidy programmes have problems of administration and policing, but if the alternative is a grossly undertrained and inexperienced labour force then it can be very much worthwhile overcoming these problems.

Developing a business culture which rewards competence

More important than the training of workers, professionals and technical staff is the development of competent and effective managers and entrepreneurs. A number of theories have placed the entrepreneur at the centre of all successful economic development and all analyses recognize the importance of enterprise and management to modern economic growth. While formal training is of some importance in the development of both skills, they are learned above all by doing, by starting new enterprises and managing existing ones.

Whether a reasonably large and experienced entrepreneurial and managerial group develops in an economy depends crucially on how existing businesses are operated. If business strongly favours family members in financing new establishments or in appointing managers then innovation will be slowed and efficiency hampered. Conversely, a business culture in which promotion of managers and access to investment funds for innovators depend more on competence than on connection is one that promotes efficiency, growth and innovation.

But business culture and the nature of learning by doing are powerfully influenced, indeed substantially determined, by the policies pursued by government. If firms are protected from all competition because imports are sharply restricted and so is entry into industry by a system of licences and permits then firms, whether public or private, can happily indulge their preference to favour friends and relatives over strangers, however competent. Moreover, in such an environment it may even be highly efficient to favour family and friends in appointments to all responsible positions. When profitability depends on effectiveness in bribing or otherwise influencing government officials it will be important to have people in key positions whom you can trust, who will not blackmail you or pocket the bribes.

In such circumstances, even learning by doing may be counterproductive for efficiency, growth and equity. What entrepreneurs and managers will learn by doing is how to get signatures on permits, how to obtain licences and how to bribe and exert influence. Of course, the better they learn these lessons, and the more adept they become at these skills, the worse it is for the economy and the more difficult it is to reverse the process and to develop an efficient and competitive economy.

On the other hand, if businesses operate in a highly competitive environment where substantial losses and even bankruptcy are a constant threat, they will have a strong incentive to back investors and hire managers because of their competence rather than their connections. Those that persist in using incompetent relatives or friends are likely to succumb to competition before too long and to be eliminated as significant actors.

Thus, business culture, and particularly attitudes towards professional management, risk-taking and enterprise, are extremely important for the success or failure of development. But this culture is quite substantially affected by the environment in which business finds itself, an environment that is shaped by government policies.

Technology transfer and development

Another important role for business is in developing appropriate technology and transferring technology among firms and internationally. Businesses have a strong incentive, provided by the need to remain competitive and profitable, to develop, adapt and transfer from other businesses the kind of technology which takes advantage of the endowment of a particular country. In countries where unskilled labour is abundant and inexpensive, private firms will be less inclined than a government or government-owned enterprises to be indiscriminate in using advanced technology, transferred from countries where labour is scarce and expensive, just because managers and engineers much prefer to work with modern automated technology.

But here again the effectiveness of private business is highly dependent on its being subject to competitive pressure. Private owners, managers and engineers, like their public sector counterparts, prefer modern automated machinery to labour. The preference for automated technology is especially strong if labour is somewhat difficult to manage, either because it resists industrial discipline or because it exerts collective pressure for better terms.

According to traditional economic theory, competitive pressure is unnecessary for private enterprise to opt for the lowest cost alternative. Even in the absence of competitive pressure lowering costs will increase profits and profit-maximizing private business will always seek the lowest cost alternative. But by now there is a good deal of evidence that private business does not single-mindedly pursue maximum profits. Even private managers often do not seek out the lowest cost alternatives in the absence of competitive pressure, especially if profits are high throughout an industry because both entry and imports are limited. They prefer well-established, readily available technology, which assures high quality with low managerial effort and a minimum of conflict with labour, government or politicians. Again the effectiveness of business in transferring technology is therefore crucially dependent on government policies and especially on whether government protects private firms from competition or adopts policies which assure that private firms operate in a highly competitive environment.

Subcontracting

One method for incubating enterprise and training managers that is sometimes considered particularly effective is subcontracting by large to small enterprises. The large enterprise furnishes a guaranteed market and can advise on technology and on management. It may even provide capital. This technique can be especially useful in a society where commercial experience is limited to a small group. Subcontracting can have great economic and political benefits where business is dominated by a limited number of large firms, largely owned by one ethnic group or by government, and it is important to develop a business community in another ethnic group.

But subcontracting is like training: it can have large externalities. Costs are incurred by a firm that helps to develop a new group of subcontractors, while some of the benefits may accrue to a competitor who then uses the same subcontractors. Some large firms may do more subcontracting than desirable from a profit maximizing point of view because they have a social conscience, a larger vision and a political agenda. But if they are subject to competitive pressure the expenditures for these purposes must be limited if they want to stay in business. (Subcontracting may then have some of the characteristics of charitable giving – good for the soul and public relations, but limited by what the firm can afford without unduly annoying shareholders, owners or employees.)

The solution is also similar to the training case: government subsidies, distributed through government enterprises, mandated industry programmes or outright subvention. If the number of competing firms is small, government intervention may not be needed. Existing large firms can get together and develop an assessment or other sharing arrangements to finance the initial investment costs of developing subcontractors. But if the number of firms is large, then an outside agency like government is usually needed.

Accumulating investment funds

In market economies a substantial share of all savings is generated by business. In the early stages of Pakistan's development it was estimated that medium and large industry alone generated about half of all domestic savings. If other businesses are added, the total was somewhere around two thirds (Papanek, 1967). Decisions on savings are very much in the hands of business itself and in this respect private and social objectives are quite consistent: the more a business saves, the faster it will grow and the faster the economy will grow as well.

There are also externalities in business savings. The more members of the business community save and invest in the country, the more their natural inclination to compete with each other takes the form of competition in expanding one's business empire. Conversely, if others in the business community flaunt their luxurious houses or cars, their wife's or their mistress's jewellery, or their family's constant foreign trips, then competition tends to take the form of competing in conspicuous consumption.

Conspicuous investment, although defined as savings in national accounts, is really no different from conspicuous consumption. It may actually be more expensive, but contribute as little to true productivity. Enterprises may be defined as having saved and invested, but may actually be reducing productivity if they invest in business jets that are little used for business purposes, or in marble-clad, centrally air conditioned headquarters building where windows cannot be opened in a city which lacks power.

But the environment which influences how much is in fact saved and, even more, how much is invested in the country again depends very much on government policy. Whatever the values and attitudes of a society, savings will be increased if luxury consumption is difficult and unattractive, because some goods are simply not available and others are expensive. If investment is attractive because it yields high returns with minimal political risk, that too will enhance savings. Conversely, if investment is risky and returns are kept low by government controls, while luxury goods are readily available at low cost it will encourage both consumption and capital flight.

Business savings in Pakistan, mentioned earlier, reached rates of 70 to 90 per cent of profits at a time when imports of luxurious cars were effectively banned and none were produced in the country, large houses were difficult to build because the necessary building materials were not readily available, and foreign travel was severely restricted by controls over foreign exchange. At the same time, investment yielded a return that could easily exceed 50 per cent a year. The atmosphere in the business community was one of thrift and austerity. Savings and investment were high despite considerable political risk. Government policies were only one factor in the austere atmosphere, but they were an important factor.

Establishing constructive labour relations: conflicting interests of the labour elite and other workers

As long as there is substantial underemployment or unemployment in an economy employers in the organized sector tend to be in a strong bargaining position. They can always find workers to replace any that cause them difficulty, as long as government does not intervene. In the absence of government intervention labour unions are usually very weak, except in industries employing skilled labour. The results are sometimes pretty grim conditions for labour in many firms: unsafe working conditions, capricious behaviour by management, long hours and no security of employment.

This is combined in many countries with extensive government intervention in some industries, including government and public enterprises. Often such intervention makes it difficult to dismiss workers, raises their wages substantially above those paid in other activities and provides extensive fringe benefits. These and other measures raise the cost of labour in these industries far above what prevails elsewhere. The few industries which are effectively organized by labour unions, usually because a substantial proportion of their workers cannot readily be replaced, also have expensive labour.

The end result is that the protected sector of the economy employs very few workers, because labour is expensive for them. Those that are lucky enough to be employed constitute a labour elite with good working conditions. But since there are few jobs in this sector, the majority of workers are worse off because there are more of them competing for jobs in the unprotected or commercial sector.

The result is that the economy is inefficient, growth is slower and income distribution less equal than it could be. The protected sector employs fewer workers, and produces less output at high cost than it would have if workers' wages had not been pushed up by government or unions. On the other hand, there are too many workers in the unorganized or unprotected sector. As a result, their wages are lower than they would have been if some had found work in the protected sector. Their productivity is much lower than that of workers in the organized/protected sector. Almost everyone would be better off if workers were free to shift from the unprotected into the protected sector. The exception, who would be worse off, is the labour elite who have found jobs in the protected sector.

In one respect the interests of business and of the society coincide: eliminating the higher wages in the protected sector. It is organized labour that needs to rise to unusual levels of statesmanship, recognizing that there is a trade-off between higher wages for a labour elite or more jobs at better wages for lower paid, underemployed and unemployed workers. The empirical evidence is pretty clear-cut: in the rapidly growing economies of East and South East Asia there was no large protected sector and no large gap in wages between the workers in some firms and in others. On the other hand, in the slowly growing economies of South Asia there was a larger gap and employment in the protected sector grew very slowly. Significantly poverty was alleviated much more rapidly in the fast-growing economies of East and South East Asia.

In another respect, however, the interests of business and of society may diverge. Most businesses strongly prefer to deal with unorganized labour, or with labour organized under the auspices of the firm. But that can result in feelings of alienation and considerable labour strife once the lid is loosened, as it was in South Korea in the late 1980s and to a lesser extent in Indonesia. Moreover, organized labour has proved in some situations to be a more effective partner in raising quality and introducing improved technology than workers who feel they have less of a say. Organized labour can also reduce or prevent some of the worst abuses of a system with substantial underemployment and unemployment, where dangerous and anti-social practices (e.g. child labour) are otherwise hard to prevent.

Business will have more plausibility in opposing excessive minimum wages and other measures which unduly raise the cost of labour if it also supports protection for labour organizations, which it normally opposes. But here again only organized business can take an enlightened attitude. The individual competitive firm often feels under pressure to keep labour divided and weak in order to preserve its competitive edge.

Thus, government policies affect and in some cases fundamentally so, the important role which business plays in training, in developing entrepreneurs, managers and technology, in promoting new business through subcontracts and in accumulating investment funds. Therefore, even with respect to activities of business itself which affect growth, government policies matter a great deal. The crucial contribution of business therefore is in influencing government policies.

The conflict between the interest of business and of a business

It has been argued earlier that the crucial strategic decision, which most fundamentally influences the success or failure of development, is the role of government in the economy and whether government policies exacerbate or compensate for inherent or inherited market imperfections. It has also been suggested that the least successful strategy has been one in which government intervenes extensively in the economy. Under this strategy, government owns and manages many of the large enterprises and directly controls most private sector decisions.

It then would appear to be quite straightforward what the business community should do in influencing government policy: exert pressure against excessive government intervention and in favour of a dominant role for the market. The superiority of private enterprise and the market has been the dominant view of the business community in most modern capitalist countries for all of this century, and the triumph of this ideology is obviously highly congenial to the business community. It would then appear that business self-interest, the interests of society and the currently dominant ideology are all quite consistent and that few obstacles stand in the way of adopting a private enterprise strategy.

But while virtually all business owners believe in the capitalist system and the need to limit government intervention in the economy, the overwhelming majority welcome extensive government intervention wherever it benefits the individual enterprise. The business ideology is based on the pursuit of profit and the exaltation of the market and of private enterprise. But at the same time it is always in the interest of the individual business enterprise that government intervene in the economy directly and significantly to benefit that enterprise. A profit maximizing capitalist would want the government to restrict competition from imports and from new entrants into the same field. A firm will also be better off if government subsidizes its output and inputs, if it restricts the activities of labour organizations in order to keep wages low and provides infrastructure services, like electricity, water and transport, at highly subsidized cost.

Even the presence of public enterprises in the same industry can be in the interest of private firms. If the government-owned firms are high cost and the government does not want to show losses, then it will assure high prices by limiting competition from imports and new entrants. Prices high enough to enable the public firm to show a small profit may assure high profits for lower cost private firms.

In effect, both the ideology and the collective interests of business dictate support for a minimal role for government in the economy, but most firms' self-interest is best served by substantial government intervention on their behalf. With each firm acting in its self-interest, their business collectively can, as a result, be a major force for substantial government control over the economy.

Business and economic strategy

Since the interests of individual enterprises frequently run counter to the interests of the business community collectively, it is primarily by acting collectively that the business community can make a major contribution to the adoption of an appropriate economic strategy. In most societies there are a handful of statesmen of business who may support a reduction of government intervention because of the beneficial longer-term effects on business as a whole. They may support such reforms even if some of their enterprises are adversely affected. These individuals are often the owners or managers of very large enterprises, who have a broad view of the economy and some of whose multiple interests are adversely affected by controls.

But given the widespread conflict between the narrow interests of a particular enterprise and the broad interests of business as a whole, pressure from individual businesses may not effectively support reforms. Rather, the most effective and reliable support for reforms and for sensible policies in general may come from organized business groups. Prominent supporters tend to be those who benefit little from existing controls and would be better off with deregulation, such as exporters' associations.

The main point is that it is business' political role that is most important in determining development success or failure. Individual business enterprises can make a contribution by providing training to workers and managers; by hiring according to merit rather than connection; by investing in research and development, and in the transfer and adaptation of technology; by following enlightened labour policies which enlist the co-operation rather than create hostility of workers; and by saving and investing in the country. But these efforts will be limited in effectiveness if government policies have created an environment in which efficiency is not rewarded but success comes to those with influence or willingness to offer bribes. More broadly, it is government policies which largely determine the rate of savings and investment, the efficiency of enterprises as a whole, the ability to sell into the world market and to buy from the world market, and therefore the rate of growth and the distribution of the benefits of development. It is, then, the influence of business on government policy which is its most important contribution to the success or failure of development.

The actual role of business in economic strategy

Business has had a surprisingly small role in influencing economic policy on broad issues in many less-developed countries (LDCs). Individual firms have exercised great ingenuity and have shown considerable success in influencing decisions that affect their profitability and the success of their own operations. But the business community as a whole has been relatively ineffective in influencing decisions that are crucial to their functioning as a group. They have been singularly ineffective in pursuing their 'class interest' because each firm has focused on pursuing that firm's self-interest. In the early stages of development when business support of reform could have been particularly important most business owners and managers have concentrated on their own enterprise and devoted little time and talent to such organizations as Chambers of Commerce. These collective organizations have therefore been weak.

Another reason for the limited role of business in the formulation of policy has been the relative weakness and dependence of business. It has been rather ineffective because it has not been unified, but it might not have been highly effective in many countries even if it had been united. Almost by definition the industrial sector in LDCs is relatively small. Moreover, a large share of industry, and often a dominant share of large-scale industry, has been in the public sector. So has most or all of banking. Public enterprise managers have interests that are quite different from those of private firms on many issues.

But even if much of business has been privately owned and managed it has often been in a weak position *vis-à-vis* the political leadership and the bureaucracy. That is because extensive controls had as a consequence that government decisions became crucial to the success or failure of every large firm. The relationship between business and government then was more often that of supplicant to a dispenser of favours rather than of an effective pressure group.

South Korea is an interesting example. Contrary to the belief of those passionately committed to private enterprise, and despite great differences in professed ideology, the South Korean public sector has controlled as much of South Korean industry and of the economy as a whole as the Indian public sector. But since the South Korean industrial and commercial sectors are large as a share of national income, unlike in most LDCs, and are highly concentrated, there has been a basis in South Korea for a business community with great influence. The Chaebol – the huge, family-controlled conglomerates that dominate the South Korean economy – commanded tremendous financial resources. In theory they could largely determine whether a region developed or not by deciding whether to invest in that region. They had well-established contacts in relevant parts of government and in virtually all of society. Moreover, both the political and the bureaucratic leadership were heavily dependent on financial support from business, particularly from the Chaebol, to nurture their patronage and support networks. Under these circumstances one might think that the business community and particularly the Chaebol were highly influential in shaping government policies and decisions.

But it was also an important part of South Korean reality that it was government that made life or death decisions about major business enterprises, including the Chaebol. The operations of most enterprises in South Korea were heavily dependent on bank credit and their expansion was even more crucially dependent on loans at a relatively low rate of interest. It was government which controlled the credit spigot. If government decided that the automobile industry should be developed and that South Korea should support only two automobile assembly plants at its present stage of development, then credit would be available to two Chaebol for investment in automobile assembly. The Chaebol would then use their influence to be selected to develop the new industry, or to be granted credit to develop some related industry or to have the number of plants expanded to three. But they made little attempt to privatize the banking sector and to sharply diminish the control of government over investment decisions.

A more active role for business recently

The role of exporters in support of reform

In a few countries the business community has played a more active role, for some time and in many countries it has done so recently. The impetus has come in part from a change in government policy. As manufactured exports have been fostered by more and more governments, exporting has become of increasing significance to the business community. But exporters, unlike importers or those producing for the domestic market behind high protective barriers, are not satisfied with the status quo. They do not benefit from the existing control system and cannot limit themselves to taking maximum advantage for their enterprise of existing controls. Instead, they are natural and strong allies for reform.

It is in exporters' interest that the exchange rate fully reflects the scarcity of foreign exchange and that tariffs on inputs which they use be as low as possible. They also favour the abolition of quantitative controls on imports. Before the reforms of the last decade exports of many LDCs were principally natural resources. They were little affected by most government controls. But a centrepiece of reforms in many countries has been the promotion of manufactured exports. Exporters of manufactured products are a natural constituency for further reforms. For them restrictions on imports and an overvalued exchange rate are major obstacles to expansion and profits. Exporters' associations therefore tend to be a strong pressure group for change.

The increasing burden of controls

The other factor which has made for a more aggressive role in support of reform for the business community has been the increasingly onerous, costly and irrational nature of the control system. In many countries, when controls were first introduced shortly after independence, the civil service was relatively honest, there was some rational basis for some of the controls and, with a small commercial and modern sector, they were administered reasonably efficiently.

Over time controls had to be piled upon controls in order to make the initial controls work. For instance, once price controls were introduced scarcity developed and rationing had to follow. When some imports were licensed and tightly restricted then demand spilled over to imports which were freely available. They soon needed to be licensed as well. It then became profitable to set up idle capacity in order to obtain profitable import licences, awarded on the basis of installed capacity. This led to the licensing of investment in order to avoid wasting of foreign exchange on imported machinery that will largely stand idle. As this process continued delays became greater and increasingly onerous for many businesses. Corruption became widespread. But above all, as the commercial sector expanded and as controls proliferated the system became increasingly unmanageable and inefficient.

At the same time some firms grew in size and their managers and owners in self-confidence. Their subordinate position to government officials became increasingly humiliating and the regulations increasingly became obstacles for enterprises that were dynamic and wished to change and expand.

At one time most of the business community benefited to some degree from at least some aspects of the control system and was therefore ambiguous about ending it. It is now increasingly split. On one side are owners and managers of enterprises whose continued profitability, and in some cases even existence, depends on protection against competition, on subsidies from government, whether hidden or open, and on governmental favours. On the other side are those who are able to compete without excessive protection and who feel hampered and stifled, rather then helped, by government regulation. Conglomerates that have a major interest in exporting are often at the forefront of groups that are supportive of reform because they find government controls confining, while believing that they are able to compete without unusual protection.

Thus, as the growing burden of government controls creates a backlash, combined with the increasing importance of exports in the early stages of reform, a significant constituency develops in the business community supporting further deregulation.

A very clear example of these developments occurred in Pakistan in the last few years. For the first time in the history of the country the prime minister for several years was drawn neither from the landed aristocracy nor from the military or the civil service, but from the business community. Privatization became a central element of government strategy and was pursued with great determination and speed. There was also substantial emphasis on eliminating the controls which hampered the business community. Controls over investment were among the first to be substantially dismantled.

The limits of business support of reforms

The experience of Pakistan, however, also demonstrates some of the weakness of even the reformist elements in the business community. They tend to support elimination or reform of regulations which hamper business but not to be supportive of other policies needed in the national interest, but disliked by the business community.

The social infrastructure in Pakistan is particularly weak. Virtually all analysts are agreed that vastly greater resources need to be devoted to education, particularly of girls, public health and family planning programmes. Another major weakness is the very low rate of savings and the negative rate of public savings. A third problem is the perception that government acts to benefit business and the rich, but does little about providing services to the poorer groups. A solution of all three problems requires greater government revenues. Taxes on the consumption of the upper income groups are an obvious step, that would also encourage savings. But such taxes are disliked by the business community and have been opposed by it.

Nor has business been pushing for deregulation of controls that support and protect it with anywhere near the vigour it has shown on the controls which limit its investment and other elements in its freedom of action. Tariffs remained high and some import controls remained in effect, for instance, even under the business prime minister.

Another necessary element of reform often opposed by business has been the regulation of monopoly, and of health and safety standards. With deregulation and privatization, particularly of very large enterprises, there is increasing need for some control over predatory activities. Protection for trade union organization is also more important as business enterprises have been freed to become larger and more powerful. But these steps are clearly not in the short-term interest of business and have not been taken.

Finally, and probably most important, as the country moves decisively to a market or capitalist system it becomes more important to increase the reach of the social safety net or other compensatory measures for those losing significantly from reform. Substantial groups inevitably are worse off as a result of a reduction in the control system and the move to greater reliance on the market and market prices. In the short term, such compensation measures have only costs, since business will generally be expected to pay for them. But it is in the long-term interest of the business community to support policies which provide some degree of security and compensation for those outside of business who face, or at least who fear, substantial losses as a result of a move to greater reliance on private enterprise.

Of course there will be losers among business as well, most notably firms that have been profitable only because they enjoyed protection against imports. But large firms among the losers can usually defend their interests pretty well in the political arena; they should be able to adjust to the new environment as long as reforms are relatively gradual; they may well own or manage other enterprises that benefit from the reforms; and they have wealth that will cushion the effects of reform. In any case, the business community will certainly be aware of the losers within its own ranks and will be attentive to their needs. But if a backlash against reform is to be avoided, or at least to be muted, the business community needs to be concerned with other losers as well, especially among the poor.

Recent history is full of examples of reforms aborted before they were carried very far, by a backlash against the costs to large groups. The examples range from successful pressures to open the monetary tap in Brazil to the electoral triumph of Communist parties in some Eastern European countries only a few years after the same parties had lost virtually all legitimacy. The dangers of backlash are clearly very real if the hardship of reform is too severe, widespread and unmitigated.

Yet aborted reforms have great long-run costs for everyone. If some of the ground gained in the first round of reforms is lost, the inevitable next round of reforms is usually even more painful. But it takes a great deal of statesmanship for the business community to forgo short-term gains and even to accept some short-term costs in order to reduce the chances of such backlash. The long-term gains from a successful reform programme can be considerable – witness the 8 to 12 per cent growth rate in East Asia and the resulting expansion and profits of many business enterprises. To reap the benefits of such reform it should be worthwhile to accept some short-term costs; for instance, high taxes on the consumption of upper income groups. They would be designed to reduce the tensions which visible and increasing disparities in income bring and to finance labour intensive works programmes to generate an income for those who have lost from reforms.

The argument here is that the most important contribution the business community can make to successful development, and to its own long-term well-being, is to organize itself to support a desirable economic strategy. This is more difficult than it may appear because it involves business supporting some reforms that are in the long-run interest of business as a group, or as a class, but that:

- harm particular firms that lose protection against competition from imports or new entrants, or that lose subsidies or other government benefits;
- harm most of business in the short or medium term, for instance by the imposition of monopoly regulation or of high taxes to finance benefits for the poor who lost from reforms; and
- increase their costs and lower their profits by taxes and levies used to finance training, research and better labour relations.

To act against immediate self-interest is never easy for any group or institution, but it may be feasible if it is done through a collective organization of business and if business realizes that the expected benefits are large. The benefits to business in terms of growth and profit would indeed be large from successful development.

2

Transitions to democracy in European history

Michael O'Dowd

Prior to 1776 there were no democracies in the world. Indeed if we adopt the only definition of democracy which would be acceptable in the contemporary world – that government is elected and can be changed as a result of a voting process in which virtually all the adult inhabitants of the country may vote and all votes have so nearly the same value as to make no important differences to the outcome of elections – then there has never been a democracy in the world prior to the twentieth century. Even if we use what we could call a nineteenth-century definition of democracy – that the majority of the male inhabitants of the country had a vote which was essentially effective – this statement remains true.

Ancient Athens was not a democracy by any definition. Not only was the franchise restricted to males (naturally, at that time and place), but the non-enfranchised males – slaves and resident aliens – outnumbered the citizens by a considerable margin. The Roman Republic was not a democracy, for although prior to about 100 BC the citizens probably outnumbered the non-citizens, the votes were of such different values that although every citizen had a vote of sorts, the electoral process was in fact dominated by a few hundred people. The nearest thing we have to democracies were in some of the English North American colonies and in the poor mountain cantons of Switzerland. These cantons were indeed governed at the canton level by a male democracy, but they were not sovereign states, being subject to the Swiss federal government, which was itself dominated by powerful urban cantons that were not democratically governed. All the North American colonies had elected assemblies with very substantial real power and in some cases all males – or very nearly all – had the vote, but the colonies were not independent; the ultimate authority still lay with the British Crown and the governors it appointed. It follows that every country in the world which is today a democracy has undergone a transition from undemocratic to democratic rule.

In Europe and North America in 1775, we can distinguish three kinds of undemocratic governments, and more or less corresponding with them we find in subsequent history three kinds of transition to democracy.

In the first place we have the case of the American colonies where partially democratic assemblies already existed, although these were not sovereign. It was these assemblies that asserted independence in the Declaration of Independence of 1776 and it was by negotiation among the resulting 13 sovereign governments that the American Federation – the United States of America – was formed and the American constitution ratified.

A transition to democracy essentially along these lines was repeated in Canada, Australia and New Zealand at a later time, except that there the withdrawal of the imperial power took place as a result of agreement and not of revolution. The similarity is nevertheless very close, for what is special about these transitions is that the institutions necessary for democratic government were already largely in place before the transition took place and it was essentially a matter of increasing the power and authority of these institutions. We will not be surprised to find that these transitions tended to be the easiest.

We must not of course neglect to note the imperfections of the American democracy even in terms of male votes. Not merely was the franchise denied to slaves (of course – that is of the essence of slavery), but in some states it was denied even to free blacks. In most states the blacks, slave and free, were a minority of the total population, but in some cases a very large minority. Looking at the United States as a whole, the vote was certainly held by the majority of males, but there was a substantial minority which was disfranchised. The American transition to democracy cannot be said to have been complete until 1964 when the last effective restrictions on the franchise of black people were removed. This was later than the enfranchisement of women, so that it constituted the last step in the transition to democracy in the full modern sense which took, therefore, just under 200 years.

Turning to Europe, we find in 1775 two types of government (or three if we count the Swiss mountain cantons). Most of the large countries and many small ones were autocracies. This meant in theory that all governmental power and authority was vested in one person, sometimes subject to some legal restraints, more often theoretically subject to none. Of course it is not possible for a single person to rule a country and these were in fact ruled by a small minority, members of a hereditary ruling class who were for the most part owners of agricultural land. Notwithstanding the theory of autocracy, if the autocrat failed to serve the interests of this class, he could be removed – if only by assassination. Much the most important of the autocracies was France, but most of the states of Germany and Italy, Spain, Portugal, Austria and Russia were also autocracies. So, at this time, was Japan.

The other model was what could be called constitutional oligarchy, where the government was indeed elected, but by a minority, usually a small minority, of the population, very often with votes of very unequal value. Much the most important country of this kind was Britain, where under constitutional monarchy the parliament was elected on a franchise which gave a vote of sorts to perhaps 3 per cent of the male population. However, the votes were so unequal in value that the majority of the members of parliament were in fact appointed by a few hundred people. Most of the other constitutional oligarchies were nominally republics. Much the most important was Venice, but they also included the major cities of Switzerland like Basel and Zurich, the free cities of Germany, like Frankfurt and Hamburg, and the Republic of the Netherlands, which in spite of its name, was more in the nature of a constitutional monarchy, with the House of Orange as kings in fact, but not in name.

On the whole, human rights and individual liberties were in a much better state in the oligarchies than in the autocracies, although there were exceptions. Venice was notorious for its repressive government. However, by modern standards, human rights were not well respected anywhere.

As already noted, we can distinguish in Europe two roads to democracy which tend to correspond (though not exactly so) to the two types of pre-revolutionary governments. On the one hand, we have a process of successive reforms whereby the franchise was extended in stages, in each case by an act of the existing government under the existing constitution, until full democracy was ultimately attained after a considerable period. The largest scale and best known example of this process took place in Britain; but something not dissimilar happened in Holland, Belgium, Sweden, Denmark and Switzerland.

On the other hand, we have the process of transition to democracy by revolution. By far the best-known example is France and other cases of sorts are provided by Spain, Portugal and Italy. Then we have a complication which arises in the histories of Germany and of Japan where the final democratic constitution was imposed by conquerors; but in neither case did this represent a one-step transition from autocracy. Both these countries had gone some considerable way to democracy before this happened. Germany's case is the most complicated and includes at different times elements of all models.

We should first of all notice that in spite of much rhetoric and mythology to the contrary, the record of revolutions in establishing democracy is not good. There have been more revolutions in European history which failed to establish democracy than which succeeded; nor have those countries which followed the revolutionary path attained ultimate democracy faster than those which did not.

Let us briefly consider, by way of illustration, the well-known and well-documented histories of Britain, France and Germany. Transition to democracy in Britain took place in four major steps with some small steps in between. In hindsight this appears as a single inexorable movement, but it was certainly not seen so at the time and it is far from clear that those who promoted the early steps wished or intended that they should lead to the later ones. The first major change took place in 1832 when the franchise was both extended and placed on a much more uniform footing. Under the 1832 constitution perhaps 20 per cent of the male population had a vote and the inequalities in the value of votes were greatly reduced, though they remained considerable. This was the only one of the changes that took place in an atmosphere of turbulence and actual and threatened violence.

In 1867 the franchise was further extended so that somewhat more than half the male population had a vote and at the same time the inequality in the value of votes was reduced to be unimportant. While this was far short of democracy, it could well be regarded as having crossed the most crucial boundary since the majority of the voters were now members of the working class. This change took place in conditions of virtual consensus between the two political parties. The Liberals introduced a Bill to extend the franchise and the Conservatives immediately thereafter passed one which was considerably more far-reaching.

The third major step took place in an atmosphere of social consensus at the end of the First World War in 1918. The franchise was now extended to all men and some women and by this time no important anomalies remained regarding the value of votes. The final extension of the franchise to all adults took place in 1929. It is interesting to note that of these extensions of the franchise, the only one that was seriously opposed and contested at the time when it happened, was the first one. It is a matter of opinion whether the 1832 franchise was part of a transition to democracy. In a modern situation it would certainly be argued that on the contrary it was an attempt to save the oligarchy, and this is probably the light in which many of those who participated in it saw it. It is very possible that it was in fact a crucial step towards democracy, while it was intended to be quite the contrary. If we want to count the 1832 change, Britain's transition to democracy took almost exactly 100 years. If we want to count only from 1867, it took 62 years.

In 1788 France was an autocracy and following on the summoning of the Estates General, for the first time in 200 years, in consequence of the bankruptcy of the government the French Revolution took place, leading to the establishment in 1790 of the First Republic based on universal male suffrage and constituting, while it lasted, the world's most complete democracy up to that time. However, it lasted a very short time. Power was first of all usurped from the elected assembly by the Committee of Public Safety, operating a dictatorship until the Committee itself was overthrown. After a series of coups, the military dictatorship of Napoleon was finally established in 1802. This represents the first failed attempt in Europe to establish a democracy by revolution.

In due course Napoleon was overthrown by his foreign enemies and the French monarchy was restored with a parliament based on a very narrow franchise, modelled on the English pre-1832 constitution. This lasted only till 1830 when in an almost bloodless coup the king was replaced with another and the constitution was changed *inter alia* to extend the franchise significantly. The resulting 'Monarchy of July' resembled fairly closely the 1832 English constitution, which was influenced by it. In 1848, the monarchy was overthrown in a major violent revolution which established the Second Republic based on universal male suffrage. The republic was overthrown within two years by a military coup, leading to the establishment of the so-called Second Empire under Napoleon the Third. Although the Empire's constitution was not democratic, it was validated by more than one referendum based on universal male suffrage. The genuineness of these referendums has been questioned.

The Second Empire collapsed following its defeat by Germany in 1870 and in 1871, by general consent of all political groupings, elections were held on the basis of universal male suffrage. This led to the election of an extremely conservative assembly with a considerable majority of monarchists. The monarchists could not agree, however, on who would be king and the Third Republic was established as a reluctant compromise. Left-wing groups in Paris refused to accept the results of the election and attempted to overthrow the government by force, leading to the largest civil disturbance in the history of France, the outbreak known as the Paris Commune. The rising was suppressed and the Third Republic survived. In nineteenth-century terms France was now a democracy. The vote was extended to all women in 1945.

Whether what happened in 1871 was a revolution or not is a question of definition. It was certainly not a revolution on what had by then become the classical French model. It was the Commune which attempted that. The introduction of democracy, in fact, as in Britain, took place in an atmosphere of widespread political consensus. Nor should we imagine that after some unsuccessful attempts France finally made the transition to democracy in one single leap. Rather we should see each of the constitutions from the Restoration Monarchy through the Monarchy of July and the Second Empire with its acknowledgement of the referendum, as being steps in this direction. So the transition to democracy in France in nineteenth-century terms took 80 years, just about the same length of time as it took in Britain.

The case of Germany is the most complex and includes elements of everything. Prior to 1848 all the major states of Germany were autocracies while some of the free cities were oligarchic republics. A series of revolutions in 1848 attempted to establish more or less democratic constitutions, but none of these was fully successful. Nevertheless, most of the states emerged after 1848 with constitutions of sorts and with elected assemblies based on a restricted franchise. Following on the establishment of the German Empire in 1870 the franchise, at least for imperial purposes (there were very important regional governments), was extended to all males, but for the purpose of electing a parliament which was not sovereign, while a great deal of power was reserved to the Emperor, to whom alone the executive was responsible. In 1918 following on the German defeat, Germany became a republic and the limitations on the power of the elected parliament were abolished, so in nineteenth-century terms Germany was a democracy. As we all know only too well, the democracy did not last and gave way in 1933 to the dictatorship of Hitler. In 1948 when the independence of Germany was restored (at least in the West) by the conquering allies, Western Germany became a full democracy with universal suffrage and has remained so ever since.

Some especially important events in other countries of Europe need to be noted. In Russia in 1917 following a small-scale, but nevertheless violent revolution, a provisional government was established and elections were called for a constituent assembly based on universal suffrage. When the outcome of the election became known the Bolsheviks, who had failed to secure a majority, overthrew the provisional government by force, dispersed the constituent assembly and established the Communist dictatorship which lasted until 1991.

In Spain in 1936 following on municipal elections based on a broad franchise, a violent, but small-scale revolution overthrew the monarchy and established a republic based on universal suffrage. This republic, as is well known, was overthrown by the forces of the right under General Franco. It is at least arguable that it was also in the process of being overthrown by the forces of the left and that the Spanish Civil War was essentially between two undemocratic alternatives. Be that as it may, the dictatorship of General Franco lasted until 1976 when, following the death of Franco, the monarchy was restored and Spain made a smooth constitutional transition to democracy.

In Portugal in 1975 a violent, but small-scale revolution overthrew the dictatorship of Dr Salazar and, after a period of relatively minor disorder, a democracy was successfully established. This is one of the very few examples in Europe of democracy successfully established by revolution at the first attempt.

When we ask what role business played in all these events we find no simple answer. It is rare to find business with a high profile in political events in the nineteenth century and it is not always easy to discover what was going on behind the scenes; and where the activities of the business community can be detected it is very rare indeed to find it all on the same side.

We must first of all distinguish between the indirect consequences of the ordinary activities of the business community and consciously concerted action undertaken to influence the political process. As regard to the first, it has been noted again and again and is beyond dispute that throughout modern history the transition to democracy has followed on a considerable period of economic development under capitalism. Indeed, until 1990 it was possible to say that no country had ever made a successful transition to democracy which had not undergone such development.

However, in the light of the events of 1990 and subsequent years, this is no longer clearly true. A number of countries which had undergone economic development under centralized Socialism are now engaged in a simultaneous transition to democracy and to capitalism. In some cases, such as Russia and the Ukraine, the transition to democracy is not yet complete and cannot yet be said to be successful; but at least in the cases of the Czech Republic, the Slovak Republic and Hungary, the transition at present bears every appearance of being successful. It may, therefore, be that it is economic development as such rather than economic development under capitalism that is a necessary prerequisite for democracy: but on the other hand the historical link between capitalism and democracy has been strengthened by these events since all the new democracies in Central and Eastern Europe are also engaged in a transition to capitalism.

We should not, however, neglect to notice that all these countries had undergone considerable development under capitalism at earlier times, and the success so far of their transition to democracy seems to correlate to some extent with the extent and recentness of this experience. The provinces of the Austrian Empire which became Czechoslovakia were by far the most industrially advanced part of the Empire, and when Czechoslovakia was established as an independent and democratic nation in 1918 it was an advanced capitalist industrial nation and at the time of the Nazi occupation in 1938 it was the sixth largest industrial economy in the world. Hungary, while less developed than the provinces which became Czechoslovakia, had also undergone considerable development. Romania and Bulgaria, whose transition to democracy so far seem much less successful, had undergone much less. Russia and the Ukraine had also undergone very substantial development in the years between 1860 and 1917 and, indeed, in the years immediately preceding the First World War Russia had the fastest growing economy in the world.

It is also worth noting that India, the only large democracy among the poor countries of the world, does not constitute an exception. India had been developing under capitalism for at least a hundred years before it attained independence and adopted a democratic constitution in 1946.

Because business activity historically precedes the rise of democracy, it follows that capitalist business can and does co-exist with undemocratic regimes. This symbiotic relationship between business and the government clearly existed in Europe and business was able to co-exist not only with undemocratic regimes which were on the whole well disposed to it, like the French Monarchy of July or the British regime after 1832, but also with regimes distinctly unsympathetic to business like the British regime before 1832 or the regime of the Tzars in Russia or the Austrian Empire in the first half of the nineteenth century. The ability of capitalism to survive and operate in a hostile environment is one of its particular characteristics and if, as the historical evidence suggests, it is a powerful agent for change, this ability is of the greatest importance.

When we turn to the concerted activities of business communities in Europe in the nineteenth century, the picture is much less clear. Early in the century we find business fairly consistently aligned with the parties and movements which call themselves Liberal. The central agenda of these parties was a demand for efficiency and rationality often associated with anti-clericalism and opposition to establishing churches, opposition to inherited class privilege with the barriers to mobility which these imply, and strong support for human rights (although this was not always consistent).

These business orientated Liberals were consistent enemies of slavery. It was the first British government elected under the 1832 franchise that abolished slavery in the British Empire, and the first United States government that was clearly dominated by business interests, the Republican government of 1860, that was responsible for the abolition of slavery.

On democracy, however, the Liberals were equivocal. When they were engaged in demanding political rights for themselves against feudal regimes, they often used quite extreme democratic rhetoric, but when they had secured power for themselves or a share of power, their enthusiasm for more democracy was often less obvious. In Britain it was the Conservatives, not the Liberals, who made the major extension in the franchise of 1867, although the Liberals had, in the previous year, proposed a less far reaching extension. If the Conservatives' extension of the franchise was based on calculations of electorial advantage, then these calculations were proved to be correct. During the 35 years of the 1832 franchise the Conservatives were in power with a clear majority for only six of those years. During the 51 years of the 1867 franchise they were in power with a clear majority for half of the time.

Although the historical link between business and the Liberal parties was originally seen as very strong, as time went on and as different issues arose in nineteenth-century politics, the business communities became more and more divided and they appear on both sides of virtually all the big issues. The three great issues in nineteenth-century politics throughout Europe, apart from democracy, were free trade, imperialism and militarism. The last two issues were not the same. In Britain where all military adventures were overseas, to be imperialistic and militaristic were the same thing, but in Germany this was by no means true. The military build-up in Germany was aimed at other European powers and the military in Germany were themselves deeply divided about overseas imperialism. Some of them feared that overseas adventures could weaken Germany in Europe.

In France the position was even more complicated. The same dilemma arose as in Germany. The primary purpose of the army was for use in Europe and some militarists feared that its diversion into imperialism could weaken France there. Indeed, after the defeat of France by Germany in 1870, German diplomacy actually encouraged French overseas imperialism with precisely this object in view. On the other hand, the French army, unlike the German, itself became deeply involved in imperialistic adventures and some of the imperial initiatives of France in Africa appear to have been undertaken by the army virtually at its own initiative, mainly with the purpose of giving itself something to do.

Early in the century free trade tended to be regarded as one of the basic tenets of Liberalism. Indeed, probably the most spectacular and unambiguous manifestation of political activity by the business community as a whole (or at least most of it), in the whole of the nineteenth century is provided by the agitation against the Corn Law – that is to say, agricultural protection – which took place in Britain in the 1840s. The peculiarity of the situation in which this agitation took place was that the only significant protection that existed was for agriculture, so that the interests of manufacturers were uniformly in favour of free trade.

We must notice, however, that the agitation against the Corn Law took place not before, but after the change of the franchise in 1832. By far the greater number of newly enfranchised people were in one or another way connected with business and the 1832 reform is often regarded (and was so at the time) as a shift of power from the agricultural to the manufacturing interest. In fact, however, this was only partially true. The Liberal Party, which came about as a result of the reform, was a coalition of a variety of interests, certainly including most of the manufacturers, but also including an important group of big land owners. Consequently, the Liberal government, while implementing a considerable amount of the Liberal agenda, including the abolition of slavery, did not repeal the Corn Law. It was eventually repealed in 1846, extraordinarily, by a Conservative government, in a situation of agricultural crisis caused by successive crop failures. The most spectacular aspect of the crisis was the famous Irish famine, but there had been crop failures all over Europe, giving rise to high food prices and widespread unrest.

Once it had been established, free trade was continued in Britain for many years; but in other parts of Europe this was not so. In the July Monarchy in France, where the power of business in the government was probably greater than in Britain at the same time, the government resorted to a far-reaching programme of protecting not only, or even mainly, agriculture, but many kinds of manufactured goods, and France continued protection throughout the nineteenth century under all the different regimes. At no stage, however, did this represent a consensus even among the business community. There was a vociferous and well organized free trade opposition under the July Monarchy and still under the Third Republic, although its views never prevailed.

Wherever we look, except in the case of the Corn Law, we find the business community divided on the issue of protection. This is hardly surprising: one cannot protect a whole economy. Protection increases prices and these increases have to be paid by somebody. On the whole, the effect of protection seems to be that the increases are passed on until they finally come to rest on those who can pass them on no further, that is the businesses engaged in exporting, which have to accept prices which are established in other economies. The clash of interest on protection is not between producers and consumers, nor between labour and capital, but between different sections of business, the interests of labour and capital within each section being the same. So in France and again in Germany we find some businesses favouring protection and others opposing it. When in England agitation for protection emerged again towards the end of the nineteenth century, businessmen were in its forefront, while businessmen were also in the forefront of the opposition to it.

We should not be surprised then to find the same kind division on the issues of imperialism and militarism. After militarism became discredited by the two world wars, it became customary for the opponents of business to focus on the connection between business and militaristic regimes – talking about the 'military–industrial complex' and indeed alleging that the wars were brought about by business interests. However, in the time before the First World War when militarism was extremely popular, especially in the working class, the accusation constantly brought against business was that it was unpatriotic and undependable from a nationalist point of view because of its international ties. The favourite term of opprobrium was 'international capital'.

The most extreme illustration of this is, of course, provided by Hitler's anti-Semitism. Most of the Jews in Germany were connected in one way or another with business, and as Hitler pointed out (telling the truth for once), a significant proportion of the German economy was controlled by Jews. Hitler's anti-Semitism was therefore, among other things, an attack on a portion of the business community, specifically on the non-nationalist or anti-nationalist portion.

The fact is that the factors underlying both lines of attack on business were true. The military–industrial complex was real, especially in Germany, but it involved not the whole of industry, but very particular limited sections of it. The international ties and interests of business were also real, but again, they were important to some businesses, but not to others. So, some business was nationalist and militarist, some business was non-nationalist and anti-militarist.

Initially, anti-militarism was a fundamental part of the Liberal agenda and the Liberal parties maintained this stance fairly consistently throughout the nineteenth century. So, in the 1860s in the early stages of Bismarck's career, a Liberal dominated parliament in Prussia refused to give Bismarck the funds he required for his military programmes. Bismarck resorted to unconstitutional means of collecting revenue. Not surprisingly, as Bismarck's adventures proved highly successful from Prussia's point of view, this opposition diminished, but the anti-nationalist opposition which existed throughout the period of the German Empire contained both Liberals and Socialists – the Socialists no more representing the whole working class than the Liberals represented the whole business community.

As time went on the extent to which the Liberal Party could be said to represent the business community as a whole changed dramatically, as an increasingly large and powerful industrial group became closely identified with the regime and particularly with its militarism.

We must not of course assume that nineteenth-century businessmen any more than other people were always motivated by considerations of self-interest. There are plenty of examples of businessmen who took political positions contrary to their apparent interests, the most extreme example being Engels, friend and supporter of Karl Marx, who was himself a manufacturer. Nevertheless, by and large we do find the business people lined up where we would expect them to be. The industries which benefited from armaments, particularly, but not only those who actually made arms, tended to be close to militarist regimes and this was what the military–industrial complex was. Other business tended to be opposed and often very strongly so. There are at least three reasons of self-interest why business that did not benefit from armaments should be opposed to militarism. First of all, militarism is costly and they are going to have to contribute to the costs. Secondly, militarism withdraws people from the labour market into the army and has a tendency to raise wages. The third reason, however, is overwhelmingly most important and is the point on which the critics who talked about 'international capital' focused. Not only war, but preparation for war and, indeed, the promotion of extreme nationalist sentiment in the population, are bad for trade. This is the essential reason why militarists and extreme nationalists have always regarded business at large, as distinct from those particular sectors of business which are close to them, with suspicion and distaste. Napoleon's famous sneer at the British as a nation of shopkeepers illustrates this attitude.

The story about imperialism is similar, though not entirely the same. The original Liberal agenda was anti-imperialist and in England the Liberal Party maintained a stance which varied from being actively hostile to imperialism to being extremely half-hearted about it. Throughout the nineteenth century every major forward movement of British imperialism took place under a Conservative government and every significant retreat took place under a Liberal government.

Here again, however, the extent to which the Liberal Party represented business changed with time: this fact was dramatized by major political events, when in 1886 Joseph Chamberlain, himself a manufacturer, who had previously had the reputation of being an extreme radical, split the Liberal Party and brought a considerable contingent across to join the Conservatives. The ostensible issue was home rule for Ireland, but it very soon emerged that Joseph Chamberlain was an extreme imperialist and militarist on all fronts, and the newly constituted Conservative Party, known as the Unionists, in which he was a major figure, was the most extreme imperialist government Britain ever had and was responsible, among other things, for the South African war. The Liberal Party, which continued to represent a major business constituency, remained anti-imperialist: it opposed the South African war and was responsible for the granting of self-government to the Transvaal and Orange Free State in 1907, only five years after the war was concluded. Lloyd George, who was later a Liberal Prime Minister, conducted anti-war agitation throughout the war.

A similar division on the issue of imperialism can be seen in France where there was at all times a strong anti-imperialist faction, and also in Germany, although it was less visible because imperialism was always a smaller issue. One of the most striking facts about European history in the nineteenth century is that in every successful imperialist country there was a strong persistent and bitter anti-imperialist opposition.

Indeed, in hindsight it is far from clear that the imperialist countries taken as a whole benefited from the imperialist adventures, especially when we compare the progress made by countries which had no involvement in imperialism, such as Switzerland and Sweden with those which did, including, on a very significant scale, Portugal. Some people certainly benefited very much, but others carried their share of the costs while getting no share of the benefits. Whether on balance the costs or the benefits were greater, it is perfectly clear that there were large classes of people who believed that for them the costs exceeded the benefits very significantly and there is no reason to suppose that they were wrong. In

Britain, certainly opposition to imperialism was strongest among the small business sector, people like shopkeepers, although there were also large businesses which did not participate in imperialist trade. Imperialism was popular with the working class mainly because of the opportunities it created for emigration and it is probably for this reason that the Conservative Party was more willing to extend the franchise than the Liberal Party was and the Conservative Party did better than the Liberal Party under the extended franchise.

There is one more phenomenon which we have to notice in considering the reasons for the confused and equivocal relationship of business communities with different political regimes. This is the phenomenon that has been called in recent times 'crony capitalism' and which was very clearly illustrated in the Second French Empire. This is the situation where a government by means of elaborate systematic and large-scale discrimination confers major favours on particular businesses owned by people close to the regime and enables these people to build large personal fortunes. Such people are, of course, strong supporters of the regime and the favours are given to them both to secure and to reward this support. It is very easy to see such regimes as 'businessmen's regimes', and this was indeed a view that was taken of Napoleon the Third.

However, the point which we must not lose sight of is that just as much as it creates friends in the business community, crony capitalism creates enemies. The essence of it is discrimination. If government contracts are given out on their merits, because no favours are done, no support is bought. Where favours are done to some, disfavours are done to others and so the stronger the friends of the regime, the more bitter its enemies. This describes the French Second Empire which was at all times a controversial regime, strongly supported by some, hated by others; and this division was found in all classes. The regime had both friends and enemies in the working class and both friends and enemies in the business community. Its basic claim to support, however, was military, its supposed ability to organize military power and to secure benefits by victory in war. Consequently, after its defeat by the Germans, it was left with no friends at all.

Given all these complications, it is not surprising that we do not find business playing a concerted and consistent role in the development of democracy in nineteenth-century Europe. There are really only two points on which we would expect, and do indeed find a certain degree of consistency. Irrespective of their particular interests, or views, all businesses fear disorder because they have assets to lose and because disorder is bad for trade, so we would not expect to find the business community actively involved in promoting violent revolution. On the other hand, for precisely the same reasons, businessmen were often prominent in promoting reforms which they hoped or believed might lead to the avoidance of disorder. Of course, according to the myth that the only road to democracy is revolution, such initiatives could be regarded as reactionary, but the facts of history do not support this myth. Democracy came about more often as a result of reform than revolution and revolution seldom produced democracy. So, those who promoted reform in order to avoid revolution may have played a major role in bringing about democracy, even if they did not intend to do so.

The second point is that the same fear of disorder generally led the business community to uphold a democratic regime once it is in existence, provided that it is able to deliver the basic requirements of government. One of the clearer points that emerges in this obscure story is that the business community as a whole played a significant role in ensuring the survival of the French Third Republic. This fact is indicated by the reputation that the Republic had at the time of being a businessmen's regime. It was sometimes called by its critics 'the Rentier's Republic'. Of course a rentier is not a businessman – it is a person who holds government stock and lives on interest – but the relative orderliness and stability which served the interest of rentiers also served the interest of business, and also served to perpetuate France's first successful democracy.

It is because in Europe democracy did not generally come about as a result of revolution and even when it did, it was clearly only because in the particular case other circumstances were right, that we have to take seriously the influence of activities which were not necessarily aimed at promoting democracy. One of these is education. In virtually all cases the spread of education preceded rather than followed the establishment of democracy. The point is well illustrated by the fact that the Declaration of the Rights of Man issued by the short-lived French First Republic guaranteed universal free education, but this was simply not implemented. According to research which has been done in French marriage registers, in 1870, one-third of French men and two-thirds of French women were unable to sign their names. This, however, represented a much higher level of literacy than existed in 1790. Education had been developed in the interval, and the same was true in England. From the earliest days in the nineteenth century, English factory owners made a practice of establishing schools for children of the employees and one of the accusations brought against the factories by their Conservative critics was that they 'were educating working class children beyond their station'.

This concept highlights one of the major issues involved in the transition from a feudal to a democratic society. In the feudal society it was assumed that people were born into a particular level in society where they were required to remain for the whole of their lives. In medieval Europe and in some countries of Eastern Europe, still in the nineteenth century, these barriers were extremely rigid and were enforced by law. In England by the beginning of the nineteenth century, there were no surviving legal class barriers, but in the realities of society they still existed to a very serious extent as is evidenced by the criticism already referred to. The breakdown of these barriers and the promotion of social mobility was one of the major elements of the Liberal agenda and was something in which business was always found on the same side, the Liberals' side.

Clearly there was much more involved than economic self-interest. It related to a whole vision of life which grew out of trade and business, and quite different from that fostered by a static agricultural society. Indeed, the change which had already taken place in England between the Middle Ages and the beginning of the nineteenth century reflected the extent to which trade and business had already extended there during that time.

At the same time, employers had a clear and obvious self-interest motive for opposing any rules which restricted their right to employ anybody in any capacity, and there could be little doubt that the purpose of educating the children of their factory workers was first and foremost to ensure that they would have an adequate supply of people fitted for the more senior and responsible posts in their factories in the future. It is indeed in the light of present-day attitudes, a matter of extreme irony that one of the accusations which Engels levelled against the factory owners in England and about which he was particularly bitter was that they employed women. He considered that this should not have been allowed.

While none of these things are capable of proof, it would seem likely, judging by the historical records, that the crucial role which business played in bringing about democracy in the long run, consisted mostly in these matters, the breakdown of barriers to social mobility and the promotion of education. These were done partly out of self-interest, partly out of moral conviction, but a kind of moral conviction which grew up in the atmosphere of business and generally not in the atmosphere of agriculture. They were not necessarily intended to lead to democracy and those who did them, may or may not have believed in democracy, but the fact is that they did lead to democracy.

3

The impact of multinationals on the 'thickening' of civil society: current developments in the economy of China

S. Gordon Redding

> Indochina, China, Russia: Despite the large volume of investment flowing in, these economies are not backed by a solid legal and conceptual framework. Multinationals should help stimulate the creation of such frameworks. (Economist Intelligence Unit, *Business Asia*, 10 May 1993, p. 2.)

It is arguable, and regularly argued, that China is a state without civil society, or at best with only an embryonic form of it (Wakeman, 1992; McCormick *et al.*, 1993). Certain counter arguments have been proposed (for example, Rowe, 1990; Gold, 1996) which make the point that in Chinese society there are functional equivalents in family based structures, commercial guild systems, and mores for co-operation which act to create a workable form of civil society without the overt institutions of the Western equivalent.

Because this chapter deals with a theme in the field of democratic transition, and because Chinese social structures cannot be demonstrated to be conducive to democracy, it will take as an assumption that in that context, the sparsity or absence of what a Westerner would see as the institutions of a civil society is in fact the case. China is, in other words, in a pre-modern condition.

Against this background it is nevertheless possible to observe large-scale change taking place. Since the 1979 change of policy and the launching of Deng Xiao-ping's reforms, the pursuit of the 'socialist market economy' has led to the importing of a vast new array of ideas. Such ideas have commonly accompanied more tangible imports such as factories, managerial systems, joint venture agreements, products and capital; but the flood of ideas is leading to change.

The change is discussed commonly in terms of the economic sphere: new forms of taxation; new commercial laws; new forms of ownership; new processes of decision making. But it has wider consequences. This chapter attempts to consider those consequences by tracing a specific process of change, namely that of creating a reliable capital market, to see how widely it penetrates society and what kind of institutional changes it is bringing. The eventual effect, if any, on the process of democratization will be treated as a concluding summary.

The chapter will proceed in four sections: the issue of civil society and the notion of its thickening; the societal context of China; the organizing of a capital market; wider implications for institutions, civil society and democracy.

Much of the empirical information will be drawn from the proceedings of a conference held in Beijing in September 1992 at which the State Commission for Restructuring the Economic System and the Stock Exchange of Hong Kong discussed the development of a 'healthy shareholding system'. The speakers represented a large number of multinational merchant banks, accounting firms, lawyers, professional bodies and institutions. Their role was to make clear the conditions and processes involved in a modern financial market. The clear implication is a form of societal technology transfer which would eventually make the capital market system of China more complex, more sophisticated, more widely accessible and probably very much more active. This in turn would sponsor related developments in professionalizing, in education, and in the growth of supporting institutional structures. It is this 'thickening' process which is the object of study.

The 'thickening' of civil society

The idea of civil society can be traced to Locke's treatises on civil government: the core of the idea is that individuals are prepared to enter into society with each other, and to subject themselves to the authority of that society, in the pursuit of two main purposes; the achievement of a form of equality based on the symmetric reciprocity of strangers, and hence the escape from the cruder, hierarchical state of nature; and the achievement of social order as an antidote to uncertainty and insecurity.

One of Locke's assumption was that escape from the state of nature meant escape from being subject to the power of another without consent, and thus the democratic principle was enshrined at the outset of the idea.

In operational terms the making of a civil society, often over centuries, entails the construction, by freely co-operating individuals, of institutions which lie between the individual and the state. These institutions have the function of providing order and of representing widespread interests of people who would otherwise be strangers. The family is thus not one such institution, and civil society is outside it.

In the sphere of capital markets, the most common of such civil society institutions are the following:

- self-governing stock exchange councils;
- stock exchange membership systems;
- a free financial press;
- accounting and finance professions;
- legal professions;
- educational accreditation systems.

The actors making use of such a structure are also in some sense part of it and include:

- individual investors;
- banks and merchant banks;
- legal and accounting firms;
- companies using capital, and accounting publicly for its use via mechanisms such as the joint stock company.

The essential function of this complex apparatus is the rationalizing of the processes of exchange and their attendant relationships. The well-springs of its Western form lie in the Age of Reason whose thinkers, as Gellner points out, were: 'Knowingly or otherwise codifying the rules of comportment of a newly emerging civilization, one based on symmetry, order, equal treatment of claims and of evidence' (Gellner, 1992, p. 136).

The rules of comportment codified in the Western financial context have been a clear example of the principle of voluntary co-operation among freely associating individuals. They have, in other words, mostly been constructed from the base and not imposed from above by governments. The notion of self-governing systems is deeply embedded in bodies such as the Council of the London Stock Exchange and the Securities and Exchange Commission of New York. Associations of banks tend to police their own members. So too do the major professional bodies and their standards boards. The rules of the insurance industry were constructed by that industry. Accounting standards are the preserve of the profession. Membership rights entail membership obligations and the sanction of loss of membership is sufficiently damaging to ensure compliance and thus effective self-government of most such bodies.

In the increasing elaboration of such systems the role of information is crucial and so too the openness and penetration of the system of communication. The role of the financial press, and of other means of information diffusion, is critical to the smooth workings of both the activities of the capital market system and of the maintenance of rationality within it.

The societal context of China

Radical change is now occurring in China in the economic sphere and it is clear that Deng Xiao-ping was driving the process. Further reforms are announced almost daily and the attempt by Ju Rong-ji to pursue further growth while preventing overheating is beginning to seem successful. The principle being followed is that of a 'socialist market economy', and the compromises this entails have not yet led to any fundamental shift of ideological position.

The compromises derive from the unresolved dilemmas inherent in the attempt to modernize without political decentralization. Economic decentralization is proceeding, but the view from the top in China is that the state itself must be maintained by central political control and without that it will disintegrate.

What we see is a perpetuation of a very long-established state apparatus with the following components:

(1) An emperor, ruling with the mandate of heaven, in other words personally representing a state political philosophy. For most of Chinese history he or she was constrained to behave benevolently and responsibly or to have the mandate removed by the people; and for most of Chinese history this principle was almost impossible to put into effect.
(2) A controlling societal superstructure designed to carry out the will of the emperor, and maintaining its power by holding a monopoly on the interpretation of the state ideology. Originally the mandarinate controlling via its interpretation of Confucianism, this is now the Communist Party controlling via its interpretation of Marxism.
(3) The use of military force to maintain societal order by exemplary punishment.
(4) A disenfranchised but traditionally compliant people disconnected from the superstructure by the absence of any ties of obligation either way.
(5) Reliance on the family unit at the base as the source of welfare and identity.

This expression in societal structures of the Confucian design for a stable state is an old model and rests uneasily with the three main thrusts of modernization; individualization, specialization and abstraction.

Individualization develops when the basic unit of society is taken to be the individual. This contrasts with pre-modern peasant society where it remains the family, group, or community. The democratic vote and a legal system independent of government are the clearest manifestations of the importance of the individual. The principle is also buttressed when education gives valuable qualifications, increases wealth and reduces dependence.

Specialization springs from the division of labour and leads to a complex fragmenting of society. In parallel is a necessary process of integration via the spread of information and the creation of means to sustain mutual trust. Civil society plays a crucial role here in providing trustworthy support for integration, for instance a reliable system of accounting.

Abstraction is the means of establishing widely accepted principles that foster such trust. Abstract principles are the alternative to depending on the authority of, say, a priest or a king, or in the Chinese context a mandarin, or a party official. Examples are the US Constitution, Magna Carta, the Code Napoleon, or a bill of rights. They do, of course, need to be widely agreed and possibly even debated, to be clear enough not to depend on interpretation, and to be amended if need be, by public process. Many of them can exist outside the realm of state documents.

The function of these instruments of modernization is to foster two main processes: the stable decentralization of decision-making power; and the encouragement of co-ordination. This latter, in the economic sphere, means the efficient pulling together of the specialized skills of a large number of people.

Fear of the disintegration of the Chinese state has led to an endemic concern with control and order and centralization. In consequence the attempts to move towards a more modern condition have been sporadic and until very recently objects of suspicion. Historically the development of local guilds, clan associations and simple forms of local government, have been tolerated by the state, but always with the right of override and the potential for interference. Economic integration has remained personalistic or familistic and thus non-complex, unless organized under state control.

In the realm of the codification and diffusion of information so necessary to a modern society, China displays signs of the perception of information as power. It is thus restricted and its distribution controlled and this puts a brake on the emergence of rationality in social systems (Boisot and Child, 1988). The role of *guanxi* (relationships, connections) in getting anything done in China is a notorious but universally acknowledged fact of business life, for Chinese or for foreigners.

The organizing of a capital market

In order to understand the way in which multinational corporations influence the building of civil society in China, this analysis will focus on the processes and institutions which surround the act known as listing. This act lies at the heart of the capitalist system and it is the means whereby a company is brought into the system of capital-raising so that the general public, and other bodies, can invest in shares in that company.

Before the act is a set of activities and after it is another set. Each of these is fostered and supported by a set of institutions, as is the central act itself. Figure 3.1 illustrates the main components of what is being analysed. This shows a set of eight activities analysable separately as components in the working of a capital market. Prior to listing the activities are one-off and sequential. After listing the activities are more or less continuous and they are interconnected.

The Level 1 Civil Society Components are the institutions identifiable as immediately involved in the listing process and its consequences. Supporting these are the more fundamental Level 2 Components, in particular the support system which supply predictable professional behaviour used at Level 1.

Before considering the implication of applying this to China, it is necessary to identify the extent to which it reflects the interests of multinationals. Whether it is a valid means of analysing the conveyance into China, by multinationals specifically, of stimulus to create and enrich civil society will depend on their 'ownership' of it in the first place.

The simplest way to consider this question is to present the institutions and companies actually advising China on listing at the September 1992 conference. This is given in Table 3.1 and from this it is clear that of the 41 bodies represented, 25 or 61 per cent are multinational firms, almost equally divided between merchant banks, major accounting houses or valuers. Of the local legal firms 10 out of 12 are Western firms employing mainly expatriate lawyers to deal with the interface between multinational firms and local environments. They could be argued to represent also a multinational perspective. If that is accepted then 35 out of the 41 bodies (85 per cent) fall into this category. It appears then that as a simple empirical fact the preponderant influence on China's rethinking in the forum in question comes from companies who are themselves multi-national and whose thinking is likely to reflect their work for many others of the same persuasion. Sponsorship of the conference by the State Commission for Restructuring the Economic System suggests that the influence is likely to be taken seriously, and its sources officially approved.

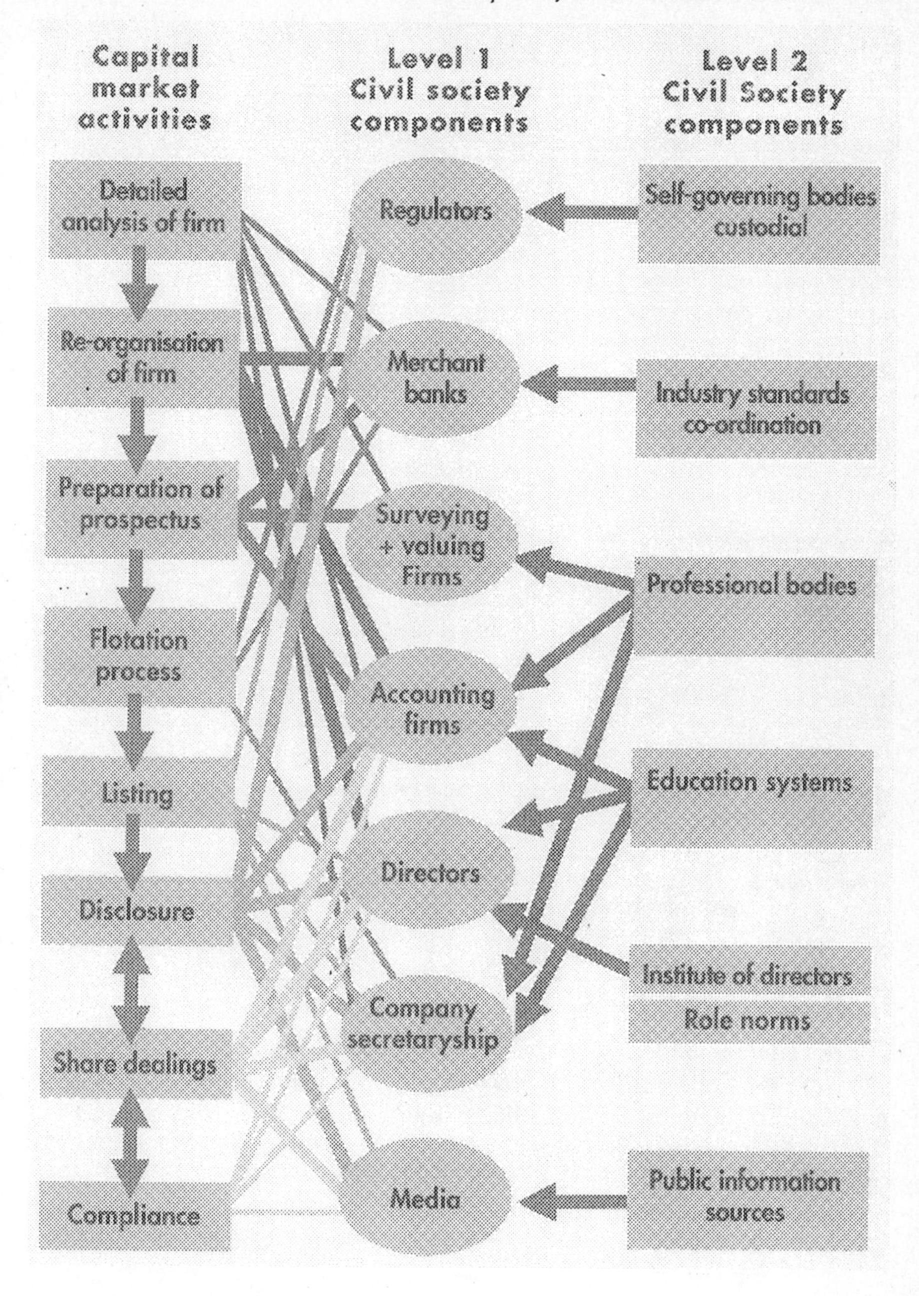

Figure 3.1 Capital market activities and their supporting civil society institutions

Table 3.1 Institutions advising China on listing and capital market organization, Beijing, September 1992

Self-governing institutions	*Valuers*
Stock Exchange of Hong Kong	Chesteston Perry
Institute of Chartered Secretaries and Administrators	First Pacific Davies
	Richard Ellis
	Knight Frank Kan
	Colliers Jardine
	Vigers
	Sallmans
	American Appraisal
	Jones Lang Wootton
Multinational merchant banks	*Local legal*
Prudential Asia	Victor Chu
Barclays de Zoete Wedd	Richard Butler
Baring Brothers	Woo Kwan Lee + Lo
Jardine Fleming	Slaughter + May
Morgan Grenfell	Baker McKenzie
Peregrine	Linklater + Paines
Standard Chartered	Freshfields
Rothschild	Norton Rose
Wardley	Clifford Chance
Schroders	Deacons
	Herbert Smith
	Allen + Overy
Multinational accounting houses	*Local accounting firms*
Price Waterhouse	Kwan Wong Tan + Fong
Deloitte Touche Tohmatsu	
Coopers and Lybrand	
Ernst and Young	
KPMG Peat Marwick	
Arthur Anderson	
Government	
Securities & Futures Commission	

Permission to seek listing

Before analysing the processes involved in listing, a significant consideration reflecting on civil society is the way the process begins. In China, companies issuing shares to be listed are pre-approved or 'chosen' by government authorities such as the Commission for Economic Restructuring, the People's Bank of China and the government department in charge of the relevant company.

In Hong Kong, by contrast, and as in most international stock markets, it is the company itself which initiates the decision to come to the stock market. From then on it is a matter of demonstrated compliance with objective listing qualifications, and the proper disclosure of information. In these respects the Stock Exchange and the Companies Registry act essentially to ensure that compliance. The principle of full and fair disclosure leaves the final judgement in the hands of the investors themselves.

Stages in the listing process

Detailed analysis of firm

The first step in the listing process is an analysis of the firm to see if it is ready for listing. What this means is that a body of institutions, specifically merchant banks, valuation firms and major accounting firms in effect sponsor it and by implication confirm to the public that its management is professional, its internal systems rational, and its procedures conducted with propriety. This injects into the firm a set of standards and their maintenance in the longer term remains an implicit responsibility of the same sponsors, a point to be illustrated later under 'compliance'.

The analysis commonly includes an analysis of firm strategy in preparation for public disclosure of the firm's longer-term intentions. This is normally done using a scientific process of justification for proposed strategic choices and thus spreads the rationality to more areas of corporate behaviour than systems of administration. It thus incorporates theory, developed in the educational sector, designed to assist in the strategic process.

In China this form of analysis remains under the control of government bodies. The creation, for instance, of a body of Certified Public Accountants is the subject of a new law enforced on 1 January 1994 and the profession is thus only in embryonic form. A mission to Beijing by the HK Society of Accountants to discuss the profession reported meetings with seven government bodies but none outside government *South China Morning Post*, 19 November 1993).

The first production of standards for accounting in China began with '10 to 15' in early 1994 and indications are that they would follow international norms and be reciprocal with those in Hong Kong.

Reorganization of the firm

This process involves mainly the directors with the advice of merchant banks and accounting firms. Its main aim is to create clear units of organization operating in business fields which the public can understand. It thus tends to move unrelated businesses into other capital-raising vehicles. It also attempts to deal with the problem of the power of minority interests to prevent a board from controlling a firm's behaviour, and aims to clarify issues of prior borrowing, third-party relations and conflicts of interest. In doing so, it might well advise on a reconstitution of the board and also raise the consciousness of board members over their statutory responsibilities. In this latter context, the role norms propagated by bodies such as the Institute of Directors and the Securities and Futures Commission's Model Code are powerful instruments of civil society.

Reorganization of firms in this way develops in response to public demand for such clarity. It thus responds to critical pressure from media commentary, financial analysts issuing advice from merchant banks, and a public informed by widespread access to information. Without these stimuli, the process in China will inevitably be also embryonic.

An indication of this is provided in the following comparison given by Baring Brothers:

> In Hong Kong, if the controlling shareholder (holding 35% or more of the voting rights) has interests in another operation other than the operation of the company, which would or may create competition with that of the issuer, the Stock Exchange may disapprove the listing application for reason that the controlling shareholder has conflicting interests with all the shareholders or request the company to appoint an adequate number of independent non-executive directors to represent the interests of all the shareholders. Under the prevailing conditions in the Chinese market, controlling shareholders (government departments) generally have interests in competitive operations (say the Textile Department may hold controlling interests in a number of textile factories in China), and these textiles factories would become competitors as market economy further develops. (CSRC/SEHK, 1993, p. 317)

Preparation of prospectus

The prospectus of a firm tells investors what the directors claim for its future, based on what professional firms guarantee about its past. In Hong Kong, the law imposes various criminal and civil liabilities to ensure that information is true and accurate. Directors, sponsors, underwriters, experts and professional advisers may have personal liability for untrue, false or misleading statements. It is noteworthy that such liability is personal and this demonstrates the workings of the professional process, in that the diffusion of responsibility for the public interest goes down to the individual level. What a prospectus is required to contain in Hong Kong are details of:

- share capital;
- indebtedness;
- parties involved in the offer;
- general information about the firm;
- trading record;
- directors;
- profit and dividend forecast;
- future plans and prospects;

- use of proceeds;
- accountant's report;
- property valuation report;
- statutory legal compliance documents.

This clearly requires the support of a large variety of professionals, each brought to bear on the process through the medium of firms such as merchant banks, but each individually accountable for the application of professional standards eventually set and governed by the civil society structures of bodies such as the Hong Kong Society of Accountants and the Institute of Bankers.

In China, the move of such responsibilities from the public sector to the private is only just beginning but is now official doctrine. It is not, however, clear how far it will be allowed to go.

Flotation

Flotation is the act of placing shares on the market and may be done in several ways; e.g. an offer for subscription, an offer for sale, an offer by tender, or placing. These vary by the method chosen to reach investors, and also by method used to establish share price, but they are all conducted by professionals. Merchant banks, regulators and company secretaries are the main actors in the process. The use of the media is also common in the marketing process.

Again, some of the most critical activities, in addition to the mechanics, involve the application of professional judgement and especially the establishing of price, and that judgement is scrutinized in the interests of the public good by the civil society bodies of the professions and the press. Again, in China, these institutions are still to be built.

Listing

Listing is the sum of all the processes identified here, so will not be analysed as such, except to take note of a wider fact in relation to China. As reported by Prudential Asia Capital Ltd, as at September 1992:

> No PRC incorporated companies have yet been able to obtain a listing on the Stock Exchange of Hong Kong because of difficulties such as failure to comply with the stringent accounting requirements and registering the prospectuses with the Registrar of Companies in Hong Kong (CSRC/SEHK, 1993, p. 229)

Disclosure/share dealings/compliance

After going public, a firm enters a new relationship with society and the three related activities of disclosure, share dealings and compliance become matters of public interest. To guard that interest, sets of regulations are enforced by legal process and professional conduct. In Hong Kong they include:

- Rules Governing the Listing of Securities on the Stock Exchange of Hong Kong Ltd.
- Hong Kong Codes on Takeovers and Mergers and Share Repurchases.
- Securities and Futures Commission Ordinance.
- Protection of Investors Ordinance.
- The Securities Rules 1989.
- Securities (Disclosure of Interest) Ordinance.
- Securities (Insider Dealings) Ordinance.

The main responsibility here lies with the company secretary, a professional role with its own civil society support system in the Institute of Chartered Secretaries and Administrators. In addition, compliance is often achieved with advice from a merchant bank. As described in the context by Wardley Corporate Finance Ltd.

> One of the jobs of a financial adviser is to advise a company on how to comply with these laws and regulations ... Generally a financial adviser would be a merchant bank which employs accountants, lawyers and research associates with MBAs. The task of a financial adviser involves principally the provision of professional opinion on financial matters to the directors or shareholders of a company with respect to acquisitions, assets disposal, internal reorganization or financing. (CSRC/SEHK, 1993, p. 371)

Within this process a critical aspect is the application of judgement as to whether transactions are 'fair and reasonable', and thus the protection of public interest. It is noteworthy also that the MBA is acknowledged as a professionalizing qualification in the field of organizational judgement.

Perhaps the most powerful civil society instrument serving to ensure compliance is a free press. In addition to the press, and its freedom, is the question of publicly available data. In Hong Kong the volume and quality of this is high, and includes what is in public libraries, in electronic data banks, in the work of private sector analysts, and in government data available via both publications and the records of the Companies registry.

China lacks such public data and lacks also a free press. It also lacks independent professions. Disclosure and compliance at an effective level still await the growth of such institutional supports.

Implications

The process described in this chapter is one of many whereby the influence of multinationals is penetrating China. Other similar influences would be analysable in the fields of technology transfer, of company management, of training and education, and of commercial law.

That it is multinationals in particular who carry such influences is attributable to two related and powerful needs: their need for rationality, in the pursuit of consistency with their other operations, especially in the home base; and their need to cope with the high levels of uncertainty found in business environments such as that of China. The building of a civil society, or the act of making an existing one more complete and more persuasive, serve to reduce personalism and enhance rationality and objectivity. It is arguable that no other institutions feel such needs so strongly or so immediately.

Consistency with other more familiar systems of exchange is important as a means of reducing risk in decision making. The bringing of order to a capital market, for instance, allows that market to be used like others. Without order the market is useless or very risky and the natural tendency of the rationality-driven corporation such as a multinational company, as it wishes to expand its sphere of influence, is to attempt to impose its own form of order.

In the wider context of a national environment uncertainty is seen by most multinationals as a serious threat to the conduct of business. They cannot read the signals; they do not understand where the power lies; they do not understand the influence processes. Nor do they know the shape of the market, the appropriate cost structures or the true nature of competition. To handle these their collective wish is for information to be available, for qualifications to have meaning, for professional judgement and skill to be accessible and for the governing regulations to be clear.

Their uncontrovertible assumption is that the further these forces progress, the greater the volume of economic exchange a society can sustain, as vividly illustrated for example in the contrast of China and Japan. Their ultimate interest is in access to that increased volume of exchange.

When looked at in terms of civil society the influence process itself works firstly, by promulgating standards; secondly, by exemplifying the institutions which create and sustain such standards; and thirdly, at some remove, by creating a demand for the societal support structures which sustain the institutions. So, access to capital requires listing; listing requires the skills of, among others, accountants; accountants require professional bodies; professional bodies require accounting education.

The position in China is that most business related decisions remain heavily influenced by government agencies of one kind or another and are thus inhibited. In the case of capital market formation, the supporting institutions are still vestigial and so too the societal support such as education.

What is now likely is that the privatizing of the economy, now moving at a fast pace, and the extensions of commercial law, will serve to reduce the grip of government. In turn, the need for alternative guarantors of order will stimulate the creation or enhancement of other societal institutions, such as professional bodies. If these take on their own momentum then more basic support systems in education are predictable.

Hong Kong is a headquarters city for the Asian offices of 670 multinationals, most of whom are there because of the possibilities of entering China. By an accident of history which make the circumstances special, Hong Kong reverted to China in 1997. Although it will be to a degree sealed off under the 'one country–two systems' principle it will nevertheless be the source of a great deal of influence on the modernization of China. Above all else, it will be an example of a society with a dense and elaborate civil society. That society has been built under the strong influence of the interests of international business.

It is, however, clearly seen by China as a revolutionary cell, and the extreme resistance of Beijing to a voting constituency of even 20 per cent of the population, and the reduction of the voting age from 21 to 18 (as in China!), indicates the nervousness over democracy in the ultimate totalitarian state. This means that the penetration of civil society will be slow, and that responsibility for its encouragement will not be the government's. It will be the private sector, and especially the multinationals, which achieve whatever can be achieved in the way of thickening a currently very thin substance.

4

Business in ethnically divided developing countries

Myron Weiner

Economic growth cannot take place in the absence of co-operation between the state and the private sector. If there is any single lesson to be learned from the economic successes in East Asia it is that co-operation between firms and the state, and even among firms themselves, is essential if a country is to compete effectively in world markets. In an adversarial environment, domestic firms will be averse to risk-taking, foreign businesses will not invest, confrontations between unions and management will disrupt production, and local capital will be in flight. In a co-operative environment, the private sector and government can work together to create conditions conducive to industrial expansion and to enable firms to acquire the knowledge necessary to compete in world markets. Successful industrial performance by firms requires that they are able to raise capital, acquire new technologies, have a trained and committed labour force, and know their markets. Governments can help or hinder firms to satisfy these needs.

How is it possible for government and business to work together in an ethnically divided society when members of the government belong to one ethnic community and businessmen belong to another? This chapter will describe business–government relations in ethnically divided developing countries and the strategies adopted by minority business communities to seek accommodation with the majority ethnic community in control of the state apparatus.

Business in ethnically divided societies

In most of the ethnically divided societies of the world corporations are owned and managed by individuals belonging to an ethnic minority. In some instances the retailers and money lenders, the 'middlemen' between producers and consumers, are also members of an ethnic minority. In contrast, the other major institutions of the society – the army, police, bureaucracy, major political parties and legislative bodies – are often controlled by members of the ethnic majority. Where corporations or retail businesses are controlled by ethnic minorities, the result is almost always public and political hostility to minority-owned corporations and minority middlemen. The reasons for the stratification of the occupational and property structure along ethnic lines are complex and diverse, embedded in historical circumstances and in culture; but the reasons why the indigenous majority is hostile to minority domination of corporations and of retail trade and services are relatively simple and uniform. We shall briefly consider each of these issues.

To understand why in developing countries so many corporations and retail trade and services are in the hands of minorities we must first turn to the history of European colonial expansion, particularly to the development of the modern corporation under imperial auspices. The modern corporation emerged in the West with the establishment of the principle of property rights. Once individuals could own, buy and sell assets a modern market system could develop. Market systems enabled individuals to take initiative and assume the risk of creating productive enterprises. The historic role of the state has been to create a legal environment which ensured business that contracts are inviolable, and that the laws and the courts protected business against confiscatory actions and provided patent protection. States also provided the basic infrastructures – highways, railways, electric power, and the financial institutions which enabled businesses to function either through direct state investment or by enabling these infrastructures to develop through private resources. In many societies, the state will do substantially more to assist and even protect business from the vagaries of the market itself. The result is that businessmen have often been in a politically privileged position. They have greater access to public officials than other sectors of society, especially if public officials believe that business needs encouragement and support.

The relationship between business and government in the colonial and post-colonial state has been quite different from that in liberal democratic states. For one thing, colonial trading companies often penetrated the colony prior to the establishment of the imperial state. In South Asia, for example, the East India Company arrived before the establishment of British colonial authority. Similarly, in Indonesia, the Dutch East India Company (VOP) arrived on the scene before the Dutch government. The company and then later the Crown provided the impetus, the framework, and sometimes the resources for the development of plantations, banks, railways, shipping companies, and industrial plants. Throughout Africa and Asia capitalism was introduced by the imperial West.

In colonial societies some ethnic groups proved to be more adaptive than others to the new capitalist institutions. In some countries traditional non-landholding trading communities prospered as intermediaries between producers and consumers; some joined with European capitalists to form joint enterprises or became producers or distributors in a global network. These new groups were derided by Marxists as members of a 'comprador' class. In many of the colonies the new entrepreneurs were immigrants from abroad – often from other colonies – who were able to take advantage of the economic opportunities (e.g. the establishment of property rights and a secure environment) created by the imperial states. The non-imperial business classes of migrant origin were able to create global financial and trading networks precisely because they were immigrants. They had greater knowledge and access to external markets and finances than indigenous industrialists and traders. Global familial and ethnic networks were an asset. The hidden hand of the market was less important than the handshake of ethnicity. A Chinese businessman in Singapore could borrow from a relative in Canton; a Lebanese trader in Lagos could negotiate a trade deal with a Lebanese businessman in Cairo; an Indian Chettier in Rangoon could loan money to a Burmese peasant knowing that he could arrange for the sale of the rice to a Chettier in Madras. Mutual trust reduced risk and networks expanded opportunities both within and across national borders. Where minorities were part of a global diaspora, they were more sensitive than purely local entrepreneurs to what knowledge was needed to compete in the global economy (Kotkin, 1993). Almost everywhere in the former colonies many of the most successful traders and entrepreneurs were (and often continue to be) outsiders: Chinese, Indians, Lebanese, Greeks, Jews and, of course, European businessmen from the imperial power. To the economist these ethnic groups were boosting the world economy by their capacity to build businesses across international borders; to nationalists they were minorities who lacked a commitment to the nation and who could not, therefore, be trusted to behave in the national interest.

In most colonial states both the large industrial firms and the trading companies were owned by members of an ethnic minority. In Canton, Shanghai and Hong Kong the Hongs, or trading establishments and factories, were British owned. In Thailand, Vietnam, Malaysia, Indonesia and the Philippines, many of the large business houses were owned by Chinese. In Burma, Uganda and Kenya many businesses and financial institutions were owned by Indians; in West Africa by Lebanese Christians; and in East Africa, the Congo, Angola, Mozambique, Rhodesia, Algeria and South Africa by Belgian, Dutch, Portuguese, French, British and Boer settlers. In Sri Lanka, India and Malaysia, tea, rubber and coffee plantations were in the hands of the British. In the Ottoman empire – a precapitalist imperial state – much of the trade was in the hands of Christian minorities, the Greeks and Armenians.

Even when businessmen – producers or traders – were indigenous they were often members of an ethnic minority. Marwaris from Rajasthan were the dominant non-British Indian business group in Calcutta. In Bombay, it was Parsis, Gujaratis and Ismaelis; in Lebanon, Arab Christians; in Egypt, Copts; in Syria and Iraq, Jews; in Nigeria, Ibos; in Sri Lanka, Tamils; and in East Pakistan, Bengali Hindus.

Opposition by the indigenous majority toward minority-owned firms is widespread. In part, it rests on envy and resentment and, in part, on the popular belief that minorities, indigenous or foreign, advanced under colonial auspices. In part, too, it rests on an element of low self-esteem by majority communities resentful that a minority community has a culture that nurtures savings, investment, risk-taking, and hard work. Animosity towards traders also rests on the view that middlemen are exploiters who make a profit by buying cheap from producers and then selling dear to consumers (Sowell, 1993). Examples abound of majority communities few of whose members are engaged in business: Sinhalese in Sri Lanka, Malays in Malaysia, Javanese in Indonesia, Hausa in Nigeria, Assamese in Assam, Munda and Oraon in Bihar, Bengalis in Calcutta (Weiner, 1978).

When minorities belong to a global diaspora, the indigenous elite is often concerned that the minority businessmen maintain an attachment to the country from which they originate, and that they may lack the 'commitment' that one assumes is present among indigenous businessmen. The Chinese business community in South East Asia, for example, is frequently criticized for its lack of loyalty, as manifest by its willingness to invest in China, thereby 'siphoning' money from the economies of South East Asia. The Chinese, however, would describe their behaviour as one of diversifying risk.

It is not surprising, then, that the governing elites of the newly independent states have often been hostile not only to the capitalist and mercantile classes, but to capitalism itself. The new elites were drawn from the majority ethnic communities who formed the core of nationalist anti-colonial movements. These elites were readily attracted to Lenin's theory of imperialism which equated capitalism with imperialism, especially when the capitalists were themselves of foreign origin. All businessmen were suspect since it was widely believed that their wealth grew out of collusion with the Western imperialists.

The majority of post-colonial governments were, therefore, hostile to business. They adopted policies aimed at weakening or destroying capitalist domination of the market by attacking the market itself. They nationalized banks and private firms, took over the distribution system, and declared that the 'commanding heights' of the economy should henceforth be in the public sector. They created, then shielded, state-run enterprises from the world economy through duties and import restrictions, and established state-run marketing boards to control the export of commodities. In some countries the majority community and their governments directly and brutally attacked individual members of the business community: Indian traders, shopkeepers, moneylenders, and industrialists were expelled from Burma and Uganda; Chinese were expelled or killed in Vietnam and in Indonesia; and Jews were forced out of North Africa and the Levant.

There were a few notable exceptions to the anti-capitalist, anti-business stance assumed by post-colonial governments. Singapore, Taiwan and South Korea were notably pro-business. But in each of these countries the capitalist class belonged to the same ethnic group as those who controlled the political system. Close personal bonds between the political and the business classes based on ethnicity, kinship and social class helped to avoid the kind of adversarial relationship that marked business–government relationships in other post-colonial states.

Business strategies

In a politically hostile environment, business must pay as much, if not more, attention to what government does than what the market does. Protecting the firm against government policies and against the intrusion of government bureaucrats becomes vital to the survival of the firm. Survival, protection, security, these become the primary goals, with productivity, efficiency and honest profit-making relegated to secondary concerns.

In ethnically divided societies where businessmen belong to the minority community, there have been two alternative strategic responses. One has been for business to work within the restrictive economic framework established by an anti-business political elite by paying what is euphemistically known as 'rents' in return for the benefits and protection that enable individual enterprises to profit, even though the economy as a whole may languish. A second strategy is for the business community to form an alliance with the political elite to create a policy framework that enables the economy as well as individual businesses to flourish. In some respects the two strategies are similar. They both entail the creation of a symbiotic relationship in which the 'client' businessman becomes the 'patron' to the politician and official. But in one case this relationship is intended to benefit the individual business; in the other case the relationship is intended to benefit business and the economy as a whole. To illustrate the difference, it is proposed to provide examples of the two strategies. As an example of the first strategy, we shall look at the Indian case where businessmen accommodated to a restrictive industrial policy environment in order to maximize their individual utilities. As an example of the second strategy we shall look at the Indonesian and Malaysian cases where Chinese businessmen formed an alliance with government to create a policy framework that enabled the economy to grow while also serving the financial interests both of the business community and the government elites. We shall also suggest that there are important distinctions between the Malaysian and Indonesian cases which may have implications for the political development of the two countries.

Accommodation to socialism: the Indian case

The Indian case provides us with an example of how business in an ethnically divided society responded to state economic policies in an effort to ensure their own survival. Though the Indian business community supported the Indian National Congress and the demand for independence from the British, it had remarkably little influence on post-independence economic development policy. Immediately after independence Prime Minister Nehru embarked on a development programme (the Industrial Policy Resolution of 1949) which emphasized state investment in the creation of a large public sector, a redistributive policy in which the public sector was given a dominant role, financial and credit institutions were to be nationalized, and a legal framework was established which enabled the government to have wide powers of economic regulation over the private sector. Three years later, in 1951, the Industries Development Regulation Act was passed which imposed comprehensive controls and regulations on the private sector. The Act gave government the authority to award industrial licences before any new facilities could be built, and granted government control over supply, distribution and prices. In a memorable quote, the chief minister of Uttar Pradesh, India's largest state, said: 'Even a bird needs my permission to fly'.

India's nationalist leadership was explicitly socialist. Its most prominent figures, such as Jawaharlal Nehru, had been educated in England at a time when Fabian socialism held an influential position in intellectual circles. The nationalists were also much impressed with the Soviet model, a country which appeared to have prospered without capitalism. Above all, the nationalists were persuaded that capitalism was inequitable, and that since indigenous capitalists were weak the capitalist route to development would only strengthen the hands of imperial capitalism in the guise of multinational corporations. The state, they believed, could be the principal engine for both growth and equity (Frankel, 1978).

The Indian business community passively accepted the socialistic policies adopted by the Indian government. There were three reasons. First, a section of the business community, led by G.D. Birla, a member of the Marwari community and the most prominent member of the Calcutta business community, argued that since the Communist Party was a potential political threat, the Congress government had to take a leftist position on economic policy if it was to sustain popular support. Birla persuaded other businessmen that despite the radical tone and socialist rhetoric of the Nehru government, a mixed economy would prevail that would permit the indigenous business community to prosper.

Second, many businessmen believed that they could personally profit under the proposed economic policies. The government's proposed import substitution policy would enable businessmen to produce consumer goods for the domestic market without fear of international competition. Moreover, influential businessmen would be able to negotiate through the maze of government regulations by providing financial support to the Congress party, and to relevant ministers and government officials. So long as individual businessmen could avail themselves of the benefits provided by the regulatory state, they believed there was no need for the business community to oppose state policies.

Third, businessmen recognized that Indian political culture was hostile to the private sector; they thought it futile to fight against widely held beliefs. In part, as we have already suggested, this hostility was related, as elsewhere, to the perceived linkage between capitalist entrepreneurship and imperialism. But in India it was also related to traditional hierarchical distinctions between the vaisya, or bania trading castes, and the higher castes. Disdain for profit and money-lending permeated the higher castes which dominated intellectual life, the bureaucracy, and the political establishment. Hostility to the business community was particularly pronounced in West Bengal, the most anti-imperialist province in the country, where businesses were largely owned by the British and by the lower caste non-Bengali Marwari community and where the intellectuals were predominantly from the high caste bhadralog communities. Not surprising, some of the country's leading economists were Bengali, and the intellectual centre for national economic planning in the early 1950s was the Indian Statistical Institute in Calcutta, led by P.C. Mahalanobis, Nehru's principal economic adviser. (Calcutta was also the centre for India's Communist Party. In contrast, the Communists had little strength in Ahmedabad, a textile city where businesses were largely owned by the local Gujarati community.)

The business community made little effort to influence public opinion against the government's socialist policies. One exception was the creation in Bombay of an organization called the Forum for Free Enterprise by two intellectuals, A.D. Shroff and Minoo Masani, both connected with Tata Enterprises, a Parsi-owned firm. Though the Forum was an articulate voice for the private sector it received little support from the business community, and was opposed by the Federation of Indian Chambers of Commerce and Industry (FICCI), the leading Indian business association.

Throughout the 1950s and 1960s, FICCI avoided criticism of the government's development strategy. Even when industrial growth began to grind to a near halt in the 1970s, FICCI's efforts to propose alternatives to government policies and to expand its role in public education remained muted. The FICCI leadership feared that an aggressive campaign would alienate the government; they were also fearful that the governing Congress party would lose popular support and become unstable, resulting in a further deterioration of the economy. In the main, the major business houses stood by the Congress government, provided the Congress party with the financial resources it needed for electoral campaigns, and continued to seek licences, contracts and concessions (Kochanek, 1974). Smaller businesses, however (especially those in trade and commerce) provided support to the opposition Bharatiya Jana Sangh (later renamed the Bharatiya Janata Party), a Hindu nationalist party, whose militant Hinduism and anti-Muslim sentiment struck an emotional cord among the deeply religious members of the trading communities.

The Indian business community was divided not only on the question of how to deal with government, but on the basis of caste, language, religion, and region. There were separate associations of Bengali and Marwari businesses in Calcutta, differences between the Calcutta and Bombay business communities, and differences between the Indian-owned and European-owned firms, all of which made any coherent policy on the part of business difficult. Businessmen were primarily concerned with their own access to the bureaucracy, with the day-to-day implementation of policy rather than its formulation. Individual business houses enjoying a high level of access to government officials gained specific benefits – contracts, licences, import concessions, and the like. They made little effort to influence the broad directions of economic policy. The system of regulations also pitted one section of the business community against another. Some industries (e.g. cement) supported the government's decision to equalize freight rates; price controls benefited steel manufacturers, but hurt many of the users who paid more than the world price. Foreign investment and collaborative ventures were welcomed by some sections of the business community, but opposed by others (e.g. soft drink manufacturers) who profited from the restricted market. The Federation of Indian Chambers of Commerce and Industry proved to be more concerned with protecting the interests of traditional industries such as textiles, jute and tea than becoming the voice of the entire business community. In the absence of any coherent and powerful voice, individual firms made their own deals with government; that in turn enabled the governing Congress party and its politicians to extract resources from the business community for electoral campaigns and for private gains. Many of the smaller firms and trading establishments, undercut by government financial institutions and by government efforts to control trade, became financial supporters of the opposition Bharatiya Janata Party.

Why was business unable or unwilling to use its financial clout – the power to invest or not to invest – to influence government policy? Why didn't the business community create an alliance with the agricultural sector, as it did in Japan and elsewhere, to elect pro-business, pro-growth candidates? Why was business so ineffectual in winning support from the bureaucracy for creating an industrial policy framework that would have led to the country's economic expansion, at home and abroad? The explanations we have offered – divisions within the business community by caste, ethnicity, and region; popular antipathy toward middlemen; the reluctance of the business community to confront nationalist pro-socialist hostility to capitalism; the traditional division between brahmans and vaisyas – are only partial explanations. By the end of the 1960s Indian business was in no position to call for a change in industrial policy, for by then few Indian firms were able to compete in the world economy under open market conditions. The import substitution policy led to the growth of inefficient companies whose costs and prices were simply too high to compete globally. India's share of world trade, a mere 2 per cent at the time of independence, declined to 0.5 per cent within two decades. Another important constraint is that business was unable to use its financial power to withhold investment, elsewhere a powerful instrument for influencing policy makers. International aid donors provided India with the foreign exchange the government needed to import capital goods for its public sector. By reducing pressure on its balance of payments, foreign assistance enabled the Indian government to maintain its policy of restricting foreign investment. And when foreign aid declined in the 1970s India was able to obtain foreign exchange from the remittances sent by Indian workers in the Middle East. Even the severe slow-down in industrial growth in the 1970s did not lead Indian policy makers to open the economy. It was not until the end of the 1980s, when India had a major balance of payments deficit, burdensome international debts, and a growing budgetary deficit that the Indian government was willing to open the economy to foreign investment, reduce tariffs, and liberalize opportunities for India's private sector (Bhagwati, 1993). The industrial policy changes introduced in 1991 by Prime Minister Narasimha Rao and his Finance Minister, Manmohan Singh, were driven by the country's financial crisis, not by pressure from the business community or, indeed, because there was a fundamental rethinking of the industrial development strategy by the country's politicians, economists and bureaucrats.

Business in Indonesia: affirmative action or crony capitalism?

It is not surprising that the Chinese business community was the target of nationalists throughout South East Asia in the early years of independence. They were, after all, of foreign origin. They were widely seen as beneficiaries of colonial rule. Many Chinese were in the hated role of intermediaries – providing loans, running small shops, and managing trade. The capacity of Chinese businessmen to engage in collective action to influence policy makers was limited. Few had close ties with the new nationalist elites that took power in Malaysia, Thailand, the Philippines and Indonesia. The Chinese also had a reputation for secrecy, clannishness and condescension towards local people. Their family-owned enterprises rarely hired non-Chinese for managerial positions. The Chinese often lived in their own neighbourhoods, spoke their own language, ate their own food, observed their own religious customs and festivals and showed few signs of identifying with the culture of the larger society.

In the post-independence period a wave of anti-Chinese sentiment swept much of South East Asia. Malay–Chinese riots in Kuala Lumpur in 1969 led the government of Malaysia to announce a new economic policy intended to provide privileges for the indigenous Malay community. But it was in Indonesia that the Chinese community suffered the most. In the aftermath of the 1965 coup attempt by Indonesian supporters of President Sukarno tens of thousands of Chinese were killed. When Suharto became President, the Chinese were a frightened community. Many Chinese had fled the country, and their prospects for security and economic prosperity looked poor.

But a quarter of a century later, Indonesia's Chinese, though only 2 or 3 per cent of the population, were the dominant force in the country's industrial, commercial and financial sectors. It is estimated that all but 10 or 12 of the 40 conglomerates, the country's largest companies, are Chinese owned and managed. The growth of the Chinese business community was in large measure made possible by the pro-business policies adopted by the Suharto government. The government deregulated the banking industry, liberalized imports, promoted foreign investment, and adopted a wide range of policies that have accelerated economic growth. The economy as a whole benefited, but so did the Indonesian Chinese business community.

Why had the Indonesian government reversed the anti-business, anti-market policies of the Sukarno regime? A variety of explanations have been suggested: the influence of the Berkeley-educated economists, widely known as the 'Berkeley Mafia', who successfully persuaded the military regime to adopt a pro-market strategy; the self-confidence of the military that they would remain in power for an extended period, enabling the government to adopt policies whose costs might be initially high but whose substantial benefits would accrue later; the fiscal crisis created by the collapse of oil prices in the early 1980s and the reduction in OPEC production quotas which forced the government to rethink its costly investments projects and to consider ways to promote non-oil exports; the growing concern of the military that corruption, especially in import licences, was becoming politically unpopular.

By the early 1980s the central political economy problem for the government was how to promote economic growth through the market without generating popular hostility to the Indonesian Chinese business community in ways that would undermine the government's reform measures. To prevent the economic reforms from exacerbating the country's ethnic divisions, the Indonesian government took two major steps.

The first was to ensure that the major symbols of public life were Indonesian. The Indonesian Chinese community was removed from visibility in the public sphere. Chinese signs were banned. Chinese schools were closed. The Chinese were required to adopt Indonesian surnames. The publication of Chinese newspapers was halted. The Indonesian government emphasized the plurality of Indonesian society, but only the indigenous peoples of the islands were incorporated into their conception of a national culture.

The second was to promote pribumi, that is, indigenous businessmen. Following the Malaysian model, government contracts were set aside for native Indonesian companies. Pribumi businesses grew in construction, in textiles (especially smaller firms that cut garments), tourism (particularly the small hotels and travel agencies), restaurants, trucking, and horticulture. Retail businesses were mixed Chinese and pribumi and there was an increase in the number of joint Chinese/pribumi firms in which the Indonesians provided the capital (through government banking concessions) while the Chinese provided the management and international marketing network. Many of the larger pribumi firms or joint ventures were owned by members of the president's family or close associates.

The Chinese were too few in number to have their own political party (as did the Chinese in Malaysia). They did not, therefore, have a formal political alliance with the government. The Chinese business community actively influenced government policies and programmes through its functionally based associations. As in India, Chinese businessmen sought to influence political leaders in particularistic patron–client relationships in which individual entrepreneurs would seek concessions from the government. However, in selective industries, namely textiles, pharmaceuticals and insurance, the business community was able to exercise an influence on government policies (MacIntyre, 1991). In return, Chinese Indonesian firms hired pribumi MBA graduate Indonesians for middle managerial positions (MacIntyre, 1991, p. 256).

In an environment in which there has been an expansion of pribumi-owned firms, the pejorative image of Chinese business has partially eroded so that business organizations have become less hesitant to openly pursue their interests. Still, considerable resentment persists, fuelled by Indonesian Chinese investment of an estimated $800 million in Fujian province. Though large firms frequently invest in other countries, the racial/immigrant dimension to Indonesian Chinese investment abroad has become the basis for public criticism. Officials continue to note that the Chinese have a disproportionate share of property in the country and President Suharto has urged Chinese businessmen to sell up to a quarter of their share in their own companies to (Indonesian) employees and co-operatives (*Far Eastern Economic Review*, 29 April 1993).

Most of the large firms continue to remain under Chinese control. Strikingly, in the 1960s the Sukarno government was not eager to promote the emergence of Indonesian entrepreneurs since 'the dominant Javanese military and bureaucratic elite preferred to deal on a patron-client basis with foreign or ethnic Chinese businesses over whom they could extract more rent' (Booth, 1992, p. 33). However, in the Suharto era, the government sought to encourage the growth of small pribumi-owned businesses through credit policies and deregulation. In textiles, small pribumi-owned firms found market niches where mass production is not necessary. The country's rapid economic growth and substantial increases in per capita income strengthened the predominantly pribumi-owned informal sector which continues, as elsewhere in developing countries, to be the largest employer of non-agricultural labour. Urban transportation, mainly small vans and taxis, also expanded with benefits for pribumi ownership and employment. Chinese firms continue to dominate in timber, wood products, real estate, commodity exports, manufacturing, textiles and hotels, but the expansion of these sectors has also resulted in a major increase in the employment of Indonesians. Nearly two million young people enter the labour force each year, the result of a high population growth rate in the 1960s and 1970s (population growth in Indonesia has been declining and is currently 1.6 per cent). The expansion of employment, even more important than a growth in wages, has given the Indonesians an awareness that they benefit from economic growth policies, even if they also benefit the Indonesian Chinese.

Only 10 of the top 40 domestic private business groups are pribumi, and all but three are in the bottom half of the ranking (Booth, 1992, p. 234). The remainder are Chinese-owned conglomerates. Given the restrictions on opposition parties in Indonesia there is no major political group calling for asset redistribution, but the government remains eager to establish its pro-pribumi credentials. Critics note, however, that since the large pribumi-owned firms are owned by close associates and family members of the president, the government is open to the charge of 'crony capitalism', similar to what developed in the Philippines under President Marcos. Indeed, one of the major political risks of the Chinese business houses is that in their effort to remain in the good graces of the regime they have bowed to government efforts to ensure that Indonesians in high positions (or their relatives and friends) have been the beneficiaries of special deals. Should a popular movement for democratization turn against the Suharto regime, the Chinese community may find itself accused of having used its financial power to promote the interests of the ruling Indonesian elite. Alternatively, to protect itself against a popular uprising, especially during a recessionary period, the regime may appeal to chauvinistic nationalism by casting blame for its economic failures upon the Chinese business community. Indonesia's Chinese community remains highly vulnerable.

A grand alliance: Malaysia

In both Malaysia and Indonesia the non-Chinese governing elites have adopted pro-growth, pro-business economic strategies. In both countries the government has attempted to balance the interests of the Chinese with policies to promote indigenous enterprises. And in both countries the expansion of Chinese-owned enterprises has been a central factor in the high rate of economic growth. The difference between Malaysia and Indonesia, however, is in the structure of the alliance between the indigenous political elite and the Chinese business community. In Malaysia political power has been in the hands of a political coalition domination by the Malays (the United Malays National Organization, or UMNO), but power is shared with the Malaysian Chinese Association (MCA) which remains in the coalition despite the government's pro-Malay stance. The alliance has made it possible for the Chinese business community to more actively promote collective Chinese interests than appears to be the case for the Chinese business community in Indonesia (Jesudason, 1989). An important outcome of the alliance is that the Chinese business community, not the indigenous Malay entrepreneurs as the government intended, replaced many of the foreign-owned firms (Bruton, 1992, p. 302), and have continued to be beneficiaries of the country's high rate of economic growth.

Following the riots of May 1969 the Malaysian government introduced what was called the New Economic Policy (NEP) directed at promoting economic growth in such a way as to reduce the prevailing disparities between the Malay population and the immigrant communities of Chinese and Indian origin. The Malay-dominated coalition government believed that the country's political stability would be endangered if the Malay community continued economically to lag behind (Faaland *et al.*, 1990). The NEP had a dual objective. One was to bring about greater equality in the ownership of assets; the second was to expand the employment opportunities and wages of Malays. Asset redistribution was to be achieved primarily by promoting the growth of indigenous (bumiputra) enterprises. Government provided preferences to Malay businesses in the form of credit assistance, advisory and extension services, technical assistance, administrative support, even direct government participation in ownership and management. The key objective was to expand Malay entrepreneurship and capital ownership. Bumiputras were given preferences in contracts if their tender was not more than 10 per cent higher than that of a non-Bumiputra bidder. Banks' funds were also set aside for small entrepreneurs. Malay civil servants were encouraged to retire early and to seek financial support for setting up businesses. Companies seeking new capital were required to set aside a proportion of shares to be sold to Malays at below market prices. There were modest increases in the capital holdings of Malays, but apparently not at the expense of Malaysian Chinese whose wealth continued to grow (Faaland *et al.*, 1990, p. 144). On paper, the number of Malay entrepreneurs increased, but some observers concluded that in effect government policies had created a rentier Malay class (Snodgrass, 1980; Faaland *et al.*, 1990). Notwithstanding the support provided by government to aspiring Malay businessmen, the failure rate among small businesses has been high and the few Malay businessmen who grew wealthy did so by buying corporate shares using loans from state-controlled banks rather than by starting their own enterprises (Jesudason, 1989, p. 195). Still, there are a significant number of Malay businessmen who have emerged as an important business lobby.

On the employment front, a 'flexible' quota system was established for the employment of Malays by non-Malay employers (Puthucheary, 1993). Foreign enterprises were induced to hire Malays and the government invested heavily in Malay education. The proportion of Malay students in universities rapidly increased. Government institutions were created to provide assistance to rural Malays and these institutions in turn employed Malays. Businesses, both state-run and foreign, made increasing use of Malay managers. While disparities between the Malays and Chinese remains great, a new Malay middle class has arisen as a result of the government's preferential policies and the high economic growth rate. Poverty levels for rural Malays are also down, largely a result of government rural development programmes and an improvement in the unsatisfactory system of rural education.

Why the Malays have been less successful than the Chinese in business is a subject of considerable debate. The hypotheses range from a history of British discrimination against the Malays and British preferences for the Chinese, to the cultural values of the Malays. Whatever the explanation, a cardinal principle of the NEP was that 'if necessary, growth had to be sacrificed for equity' (Faaland *et al.*, 1990, p. 99) though no attempt was made to specify what reduction in growth was necessary or desirable to reduce inequalities of income and provide greater opportunities for Malay advancement. In practice, the NEP had two important economic consequences for the Malays. The first is that there has been a significant reduction in poverty and a general levelling upwards as a result in the growth of employment and rural development. The second is that there has been a major expansion in the size, well being, and visibility of the Malay middle class and an increase in the number of Malay businessmen eager for government protection.

Still, notwithstanding the great improvement in the economic conditions of the Malays, one cannot rule out the possibility that an anti-Chinese, anti-business radical Malay chauvinism could at some point become a political force, one that would generate renewed ethnic tensions and do irrevocable damage to the country's economic growth.

What works to reduce ethnic conflict?

Governments of multi-ethnic societies where political power is held by the majority and economic power by the minority have at least five options for reducing economic disparities. The first is to redistribute the assets of the wealthy through confiscation. The second is to promote greater asset ownership by providing shares in firms or through facilitating the growth of entrepreneurship among members of the majority community. The third is through policies to bring members of the majority community into managerial positions or, more broadly, policies and programmes to enlarge the community's middle class. The fourth is to pursue policies that reduce income disparities through an expansion in employment and wages. And the fifth is direct intervention to provide opportunities or entitlements to the poorest sections of the society.

Businesses can rarely be neutral in the choice of these options since their own well being is effected by which options are chosen, and how they are pursued. When political power has been shifted from a minority ethnic group (or from the colonial elite which protected the minority business community) to a majority ethnic group when large economic disparities exist between the two, the resulting disequilibrium invariably generates a political struggle. Business not only has an interest in protecting itself from destructive state policies, it also has an interest in reducing ethnic tension within the society if only, again from a self-interest perspective, because violent conflict is destructive of economic activity.

From a theoretical perspective, the fundamental question is what form of intervention to improve the economic position of the ethnic majority is most likely to reduce ethnic conflict? And for which groups within the majority community? Friends and relatives of the political elite? The middle class? The working class? The most disadvantaged? Should the strategy be to provide ownership of shares in the corporate sector, entrepreneurial opportunities, jobs for managers, more employment for the middle classes, more entitlements and/or greater educational opportunities for all? And finally, there is the question not only what governments can do, but what businesses can do independently of governments.

The reality is that all too-often minority-owned firms in ethnically divided societies are narrowly concerned with enhancing their own security and profitability by accommodating themselves to restrictive regulatory policies and by seeking favours in return for providing money, assets, or jobs to government officials and their friends and relatives. The outcome of such a strategy is often short-term private gain at the cost of long-term economic benefits, and the growth of crony capitalism in which close associates of the power elites become private beneficiaries.

There is, however, a case for a set of policies akin to those pursued by Malaysia, a set of pro-growth economic politics combined with a variety of measures intended principally to benefit the middle classes. The classic argument for reducing ethnic conflict by promoting the middle classes of the disaffected community has been put forth by Albert Hirschman in a famous article on what he called the 'tunnel effect' (Hirschman, 1973). Hirschman argued that a community will accept inequality if it sees that some members of its own community have become substantially better off. The benefit may be psychological: individual self-worth is enhanced when members of one's community have moved into a visibly well-off position (Horowitz, 1985) or it may lead, in Hirschman's terms, to a belief that in time one's own children will be better off.

However, minority-owned firms often find it difficult to incorporate members of the ethnic majority into senior managerial positions. Business culture is generally not conducive to a policy of reaching out to incorporate previously excluded ethnic groups into managerial positions or, for that matter, to share equity. Many large businesses in developing countries are family-owned enterprises. Professionalization of management has often meant ensuring that family members recruited into key managerial posts have professional engineering or management degrees, not that these positions are open to those outside the family. And when firms are not family enterprises, top managers are not comfortable recruiting ethnic outsiders into senior positions, preferring instead to hire those who have similar social class and educational backgrounds. Nor do companies prize ethnic diversity in top management since what they seek is a team-like structure of like-minded individuals with shared values.

Minority-owned businesses in ethnically divided societies do, however, give attention to the establishment of close ties with the political establishment. As discussed earlier, in return for protection and favours (public works contracts, licences, etc.), the business community often provides the political elite with financial support. Where the minority community is itself reasonably large, the business elite can also play a role in mobilizing and delivering electoral support to the government, as the Chinese elite does in Malaysia. Over the years, however, a web of mutual expectations and obligations can be created that binds businessmen and government officials together even though they come from different and even historically antagonistic communities. In time, businessmen recognize that they must move sections of the political elite into visible positions in ownership and management. Indeed, in a society in which income disparities are wide, one effective way to reduce ethnic conflict is to enhance the economic position of members of the political elite. An expansion of the economically well-off middle class within the majority ethnic community can serve to reduce popular hostility to minority-owned businesses and thereby ease the efforts of bureaucrats and politicians to adopt a pro-business stance. The minority business community thus has an interest in promoting a visibly economically well-off middle class elite within the majority ethnic community. The down-side is that a cosy, symbiotic relationship between business and government can create a system of crony capitalism which ultimately becomes disadvantageous to both communities.

What role, if any, can government or business play in promoting entrepreneurship within the majority community? There are a variety of measures that can be adopted, though each has its problems. One is through a system of preferences in the allocation of contracts by government, a policy widely used by the governments of Malaysia and Indonesia to promote businesses owned by members of the majority community. A similar policy is in place in the United States for *minority* businesses in what is known as business 'set-asides'. Starting in the 1970s the United States government established programmes to benefit minority business enterprises (MBEs) and women's business enterprises (WBEs). In 1989 about $8.65 billion was awarded to MBEs in federal set-asides, including $3.5 billion in a Small Business Administration programme (LaNoue, 1992). Additionally, 10 per cent of all Federal Highway Administration and other transportation agencies' expenditures were to go to 'disadvantaged' businesses; and 5 per cent of defence procurement contracts were set aside for exclusive bidding by disadvantaged businesses. State and local governments have also created their own set-aside programmes, particularly in awarding construction contracts. These programmes have come under attack as violations of the Equal Protection clause of the Constitution; there have been controversies over the initial exclusion of Asian-American business concerns; and there have been objections that the programme created sheltered markets for inefficient firms which thereby raised the cost of public contracts since 'disadvantaged' firms generally submitted quotes that were 10 per cent higher than firms owned by white males. There has, however, been a marked increase in the number of black-owned, Hispanic-owned and women-owned firms in the United States, some due to the set-aside programmes, though some may also be the result of a general growth in the economy and improved economic opportunities for women and minorities.

In the United States a few white-owned businesses have been promoting the development of minority-owned businesses. A report in a leading business journal (*Nation's Business*, 1992) described the steps taken by some white-owned businesses: (1) by buying from minority-owned businesses and investing in them, sometimes by designating a portion of their subcontracts to minority-owned firms; (2) providing support for minority economic education, including the funding of pilot programmes that offer training in entrepreneurship for inner city youth and the training of investment managers in minority-owned pension investment companies; (3) establishing personal relationships so that a network is established which enables managers and owners of white-owned and minority-owned firms to know one another; (4) providing grants and loans by businesses to community development groups which provide start-up capital for new minority-owned business and offering them technical guidance. How many of these steps have actually been adopted by businesses in the United States is unclear, nor do we have any reports of similar policies adopted by firms in developing countries, but these policies are suggestive of measures business can take to promote the growth of enterprises from disadvantaged communities.

Throughout the world, small manufacturing firms have played an important role in industrial development. It has been widely noted that in Japan, Korea, Taiwan, Italy, Chile and other high-growth countries, small firms create a large proportion of industrial employment and contribute substantially to exports. Small firms have often been effective in innovating new products and are able to establish niches in highly competitive markets. They are often more flexible than large firms in adjusting to highly volatile consumer markets. In business schools and in economics departments older notions of economies of scale and mass production have given way to a recognition of the importance of what has come to be called 'flexible-specialization' (Piore and Sabel, 1984). Small firms are, however, often handicapped by a lack of capital, limited access to new technologies, a lack of information about new export markets, and the costs of marketing. There has, therefore, been an interest in how governments and large businesses can assist small industrial firms and how these firms can organize into effective associations to further their collective interests.

It is in this context of understanding the importance of small firms for industrial growth, employment, and exports, that large ethnic minority-owned businesses need to address the question of how to promote a diffusion of ownership and management among small industrial firms, among retail and management among small industrial firms as well as among retail and wholesale outlets within the majority community.

In the short run minority-owned businesses can prosper by establishing close ties to the dominant political elite. For this reason, businessmen often throw their weight (and their money) behind a civilian or military authoritarian leadership. But in the longer run business runs the risk of being too closely associated with the particular political group holding power. Moreover, even to retain support from the existing political establishment business needs a strategy for broadening its base of support within the ethnic majority. Expanding property ownership by members of the ethnic majority in small industries, in marketing, and in the service sectors of the economy is one promising strategy. It is good for the ethnic minority; it is good for members of the majority community; and it is good for the economy as a whole.

5

Can business associations contribute to development and democracy?[1]

Richard F. Doner, Ben Ross Schneider and Ernest J. Wilson III

This chapter provides an initial framework and set of hypotheses for the comparative study of business associations in developing countries. We begin by defining associations and exploring their functions and structural characteristics. We then explore hypotheses concerning the principal questions of the chapter: How do business associations affect economic policies and growth and politics and the democratization process? Finally, we identify factors accounting for differences among associations.

Empirical and theoretical developments make a comparative understanding of business associations in developing countries both increasingly necessary and possible. The numbers, diversity, sophistication and influence of associations in developing countries (and monographic literature on them) have increased significantly in the past several decades. Many analysts assume that private sectors will fill the voids left by shrinking states throughout the developing world. Private sector roles should also expand in countries attempting to promote manufactured exports. The crucial questions are whether private sectors are up to the role assigned to them, and the degree to which firms act collectively to meet these new economic challenges.

Recent studies of economic growth in North East Asia have also raised appreciation of collective private sector roles. A more sophisticated appreciation of the limits of 'strong' states in the East Asian Newly Industrialized Countries (NICs) has directed attention to the economic contribution of private sector institutions such as groups, networks and business associations in that region (Doner, 1992; Moon and Prasad, 1993). The lesson of the NICs may thus be that effective integration into the global capitalist economy requires a delicate combination of liberalization in state policies and greater institutionalization of business and the rest of society. In this context, associations can help 'to enlarge a country's repertoire of policy alternatives ...' and compensate for the inevitable shortcomings of states and markets (Streeck and Schmitter, 1985, pp. 15, 17).

This tentative conclusion is reinforced by a growing belief that the decline in both the credibility of Keynesian macro-economic policies and the capacity of states to implement such reflationary measures is not ushering in the triumph of strictly free markets. Voluntary, free, legally enforceable contractual exchanges among unrelated individual or corporate actors holding separate property rights are neither ubiquitous nor universally more efficient than organized markets. We are instead finding a wide range of institutions designed to fulfil capitalism's need for *governance*, i.e. 'coordination between a multitude of actors with diverse and, often, conflicting interests'.[2] Such institutions include not just states and corporate hierarchies, but networks and associations of workers and capitalists. A corollary of sensitivity to the need for economic governance is the recognition that the market vs. hierarchy vs. community trichotomy does not capture the range of institutions that contribute to economic stability much less dynamic growth. Markets can fail to provide collective or club goods necessary to economic growth and structural change. States are often weak in policy implementation. And communities often lack the means 'to mobilize resources above and beyond what can be obtained on a voluntary basis' (Streeck and Schmitter, 1985, p. 24).

Finally, the need and opportunity for greater understanding of business associations emerges from greater weight analysts have begun to give to *sectors* in economic growth.[3] The need for a sectoral or 'meso' focus is suggested by weaknesses in the neo-corporatist arrangements of Western Europe. The focus of these arrangements was largely on the national level where states and peak associations negotiated agreements on macro-economic policies. New conditions of globalization and industrial restructuring have made such peak agreements both more difficult to achieve and less suitable to competitive markets. The need for more flexible production systems in developing as well as industrialized countries seems to demand policy responses and consensus-building at levels of the economy where business associations are often quite active.

The role of business associations in bringing down authoritarian regimes and bolstering successor democracies merits further examination. Big business was often visible in coalitions that brought authoritarian regimes down, but the specific role of business associations in this process is less clear (see Bartell and Payne, 1994). As in the case of economic liberalization, the removal of authoritarian repression has increased expectations of business associations. The most recent wave of democratization again popularized Tocqueville's dictum that if people want to be governed democratically they must learn to associate. More specifically, the growth of participation in autonomous, voluntary associations 'has become a major means for the limitation of state power and the creation from below of an informed efficacious, vigilant citizenry' (Diamond, 1988, p. 26). Business associations may be key to post-transition stability, governability, and strengthening of civil society.

None of the preceding is to deny that associations can and often do stifle economic growth or undermine democracy. Business associations can and do engage in price gouging, create and seek rents, and raise entry barriers to new competitors through collusion and other strategies. Indeed, the social sciences have traditionally emphasized the negative aspects of associational life. Sociologists have stressed interest associations' tendency to become alienated from members' values; political scientists have viewed associations as components of iron triangles and thus as threats to liberal democracy; and economists have emphasized the ways in which trade associations, operating as cartels and distributive coalitions, obtain rents and allocate resources sub-optimally. It has been argued that institutions such as business associations are primarily distributive and designed to provide strategic advantage to particular interests. Whether those institutions are socially or economically efficient is a separate question (Knight, 1992). Such criticisms are common in the more specialized literature on development where the dominant paradigms have, with minor exceptions, accepted the state–market dichotomy and have consequently neglected the existence and potential contributions of business associations.[4]

These negative views are not so much mistaken, we believe, as they are one-sided.[5] Our approach is to explore associations' potential for controlling or offsetting the negative consequences (externalities) of states, markets and communities (Shreeck and Schmitter, 1985). The impact of business associations on democracy and development may in a majority of cases not be benign. However, there are enough instances of positive contributions to make it worthwhile trying to understand more systematically why these minority cases differ. Moreover, since business associations are a universal feature of capitalist society, it is less fruitful to speculate on how the political economy would function without them than to assume they will be powerful participants and find out what makes them part of the solution.

Definitions and dimensions of variation

For our purposes, business associations are long-term organizations with formal statutes in which the members are individual business people, businesses, or other associations. These associations are distinct from commercial organizations in that the member businesses are not necessarily linked by ownership and contractual ties. Members of an association may well have such ties with each other. However, our principal concern is to distinguish associations from other organizations based on mutual ownership (such as Japan's keiretsu or Korea's Chaebol) and from networks of enterprises based on ethnicity and/or contractual ties (such as those central to Taiwan's economy). Our definition of business associations includes Chambers of Commerce, industry associations, international trade associations, employers' associations, religious groups such as those of Catholic businessmen often found in Latin America, cultural or immigrant groups like the Chinese associations in South East Asia, business think-tanks and policy institutes, and more explicitly partisan or ideological organizations. To meet our definition, the broader religious, cultural, and political organizations must exclude non-business members.

The activities of business associations can be analytically divided into 'logics' of membership, influence, and implementation.[6] The logic of membership involves economic governance of and by members in which associations provide collective goods such as industry standards, collective bargaining, or information on export markets. The logic of influence involves efforts to sway public policies through elections, lobbying, and/or participation in state-sponsored consultative groups. In implementation activities, business associations mobilize and monitor members to execute public policies. In practice, most associations pursue a mix of these activities though the mix varies across associations and over time within associations.

Business associations also vary along several organizational dimensions.[7] Associations differ first with regard to the *scope* of the economy encompassed. Some associations include only firms or individuals specializing in the same product line such as the Taiwan Cotton Textile Association and Taiwan Synthetic Fibres Association. Others are broader, incorporating members from different points of an industry's production chain such as the Taiwan Textile Federation and the Associations of Metalwork Firms and Wood Products manufacturers in Chile (Perez-Aleman, personal communication, 1994). Still others are peak associations of bankers, agricultural interests, traders or manufacturers, such as the Federation of Malaysian Manufacturers. Such groups can also operate at a multinational level as represented in the ASEAN Automotive Federation and other industry 'clubs' within the Association of South East Asian

Nations. A fourth level encompasses almost all firms in a national economy, such as the Philippines Chamber of Commerce and Industry or the Business Co-ordinating Council in Mexico. And finally, some associations are industry-wide but limited to firms of specific sizes, geographic location or ethnicity, such as the Federation of Filipino-Chinese Chambers of Commerce and other ethnic Chinese associations in South East Asia (Lim, 1989).

Association membership can be more or less *inclusive* or *dense.* Inclusiveness refers to the proportion of an industry's output produced by members.[8] Thus, the Thai Auto Parts Manufacturers' Association represents a minority of the industry's firms due to competition from a rival association backed by auto assemblers.

Finally, associations may be categorized with regard to *resources,* that is the size and instruments of their staff. The budgets of business associations are typically small relative to the disposable income of member firms but enormous compared to budgets of associations of other social groups. But due to factors discussed below, even associations operating at the same level differ with regard to available resources. Association funds allow many associations to collect and disseminate information in influential ways. Business associations typically hire top economists. During the 1950s, for example, economists for Brazil's National Industrial Confederation were instrumental in devising and disseminating a compelling technical rationale for import substituting industrialization (Bielschowsky, 1988). More recently Sao Paulo's Instituto Liberal (a business association by funding if not necessarily by its exclusively business membership) published hundreds of thousands of comic books which define its conceptions of day-to-day liberal practice. By contrast, few if any associations in Africa have the resources to mount such campaigns.

Lastly, the capacity associations have to induce or coerce compliance also varies. As noted, some peak associations are loose co-ordinating committees with little influence over member groups, whereas others can make binding commitments that member associations merely ratify. This variation is primarily a function of the association's resources, inclusiveness, and coherence, and thus the selective benefits it controls. When exclusion from the association is costly, then peak associations can make more authoritative decisions, enforce compliance and impose sacrifices. When exclusion is costless, peak associations often express little more than the lowest common denominator of interests such as defence of property rights and low taxes on profits.

An intermediate case involves associations whose extensive resources are provided by the state. Peak associations in South Korea are financially self-supporting, but their leadership has traditionally come from the state elite and their financial strength depended on selective credit to highly leveraged member firms. And although their leadership by a small number of large firms would seem to indicate some strength in leadership, these small numbers also facilitate state control and monitoring of the association itself.[9]

In principle, these four organizational features influence the degree to which an association fulfils its logics of membership, influence, and implementation. For example, higher-level encompassing association (wide scope) theoretically take a more multi-sectoral or 'state-like' view of the economy and are therefore more influential and better interlocutors in implementing economy-wide macro and industrial policies.[10] Thus, the Taiwan Textile Federation has alerted the Taiwanese government to problems in the industry's overall production structure by showing the weakness of its dyeing and finishing facilities and helping to identify firms willing to invest in these areas (Wade, 1990, p. 281). As we shall see, however, even narrowly based organizations can promote general efficiency under specific conditions. More generally, greater scope, density, resources, and capacity to get members to comply all enhance an association's influence, though in different ways. Resources, density, and compliance mechanisms are crucial to the governance and implementation functions of associations. Scope may or may not be relevant to governance and implementation, depending on the issue.

An important assumption of this chapter should now be obvious: formal organization matters with regard to the interests and impact of business. For some, business gets its way whether it is organized or not and can pressure the government and aggregate interests just as well through informal means.[11] Others argue that business exercises structural power through the economic resources it controls and social hegemony, both of which render formal organization superfluous. We argue in contrast that effective formal organization shapes what it is that business wants and its capacity to exercise influence. Formal organization affects interest intermediation, dispute resolution, and the capacity for collective action in the business community.

Business associations and economic growth

Associations can influence economic growth through their membership, implementation and influence activities. Probably the most crucial component of membership-related governance functions is the provision of collective goods such as basic security, product standards, market information, price stabilization, development and transfer of technology, training programmes, legal services, and allocation of export quotas. In cases of extreme political uncertainty, associations can provide protection of members' basic property rights. According to one analyst, African associations have historically emphasized the defence of their members from predatory government regulation (Lucas, 1993).

In more stable capitalist orders, associations move beyond the defence of property rights to promote efficiency and flexibility. Some collective goods are more 'horizontal' in that they serve the interests of firms at one particular point in the production process. Associations often attempt to attenuate fluctuations in prices and demand and thereby allow firms to become more efficient without hurting consumers. For example, during the 1950s Thailand's Board of Trade, a peak association of agricultural export merchants, organized its members to develop and adhere to product standards and to avoid cut-throat competition. Since agriculture dominated the economy and agricultural exports accounted for a major proportion of state revenues, the Board's success in these efforts was critical to Thailand's early economic growth (Doner and Ramsay, 1993). Similarly, the Brazilian association of automobile parts firms (Sindipecas), helped to generate exports by stabilizing domestic market prices and thus shifting fixed costs to the domestic market (Addis, 1993). The secure domestic market provided firms with funds to invest in order to become internationally competitive. In Nigeria, an association took over the function of disbanded, state commodity boards to ensure that groundnut farmers would not be victimized by unstable prices offered by millers (Lucas, 1993, p. 212).

Beyond managing factor and product markets, associations can provide crucial services that constitute quasi-public goods. For example, several industry associations in Latin America have created special services for small firms that could not hire the legal and administrative experts to comply with the reams of regulations and bureaucratic procedures. In Brazil, the government transfers a payroll tax to industry associations that then run training programmes of their design for workers.[12]

A final example concerns efforts by the Taiwan Cotton Spinners' Association to contend with a rash of bankruptcies and a small domestic market. The TCSA adopted a Contract of Co-operation from Japanese practices.[13] The contract involved agreements among all members to reduce total production, to export 60 per cent of production, and to purchase cotton at set prices. The association also organized members to establish a textile technology college and co-ordinated the supply of raw materials during periods of shortages (Kuo, 1990, pp. 104–110).

Business associations can also provide collective goods more 'vertically' in that the goods serve firms at different but mutually dependent points in the production chain of an industry. Various Thai textile associations are combining efforts to improve the country's educational facilities for textile engineers and technicians.[14] These associations are also co-operating to expand production in an area critical to the whole industry but historically weak in Thailand – dyeing and printing. This involves developing plans and sharing costs for an expansion of wastewater treatment. In Chile, associations of small and medium-sized firms actually include firms at different points of the production and export process. These groups have provided information of quality standards and support for local technological development (Perez-Aleman, personal communication, 1994).

Perhaps the most important vertical governance function is the resolution of conflicts between upstream and downstream firms. Where inter-firm links are highly formal and arm's length, upstream firms may simply not be aware of their downstream clients' needs. In these cases, associations can enhance information flows and strengthen ties among firms. For example, in stabilizing relations with downstream clients, the auto assemblers, Brazil's Sindipecas created a stronger basis for long-term investment by the suppliers themselves.

In other cases, however, conflicts may result less from information shortages than from more fundamental differences in interests and political position. The Nigerian association that understood commodity board functions found itself in deep conflict with 'downstream' groundnut millers. The millers were part of a government agency that had hoped to benefit from a bumper crop by purchasing groundnuts from farms at prices below those offered by the association. The association refused to lower its prices but was subsequently punished when the government refused to buy its wheat (Lucas, 1993, p. 213).

Upstream–downstream conflicts often focus on the trade regime. Upstream firms favour protection for their products whereas downstream firms prefer free access to imported inputs. The resolution of these differences in the Taiwan textile case indicates the potential role of associations:

> The weaving industry supported the liberalization of yarn imports, while the spinning industry resisted it. With the help of state intermediation, a compromise was worked out. The TCSA agreed to lower the price and stabilize the supply of yarn in exchange for abandoning the liberalization proposal. (Kuo, 1990, p. 108).

In Austria, textile importers and producers resolved an intense conflict within the peak associations. This is one example of the containment of conflict that generally allows the government in Austria to respond more flexibly to economic crises (Katzenstein, 1984, pp. 191–192).

Associations in many countries perform somewhat similar functions through the provision of import referrals. Groups of upstream firms in Brazil, South Korea, Taiwan and elsewhere provide information on their capacity to provide particular inputs. Where these are not available, downstream firms are permitted to import the goods (Wade, 1990; Addis, 1993). Perhaps even more important, by contributing to exchanges of information and resources between both sides, these negotiations often help to upgrade domestic input production.

During the NAFTA negotiations Mexican businesses organized themselves by production chains of upstream and downstream firms in order to work out a common position before meeting with government negotiators. The intense pressure of the treaty negotiations gave upstream and downstream producers a strong incentive to iron out disputes before entering discussions with the government.[15]

In providing collective goods, business associations can also help to *implement* state policies in at least three general areas: long-term strategies to promote exports; shorter-term macro-economic stabilization; and the day-to-day administration of various state interventions. Business associations have made several important contributions to the export strategy adopted by South Korea. First, Korean associations helped to socialize the costs of information about export markets. In so doing, they not only reduced the entry barriers to volatile export markets but also helped to 'nationalize' exports by circumventing Japanese trading companies.[16] Second, the associations provided detailed information on the supply capacities of their members and thus helped the state to identify gaps in production structures. Finally, the associations were an important institutional tool for achieving export targets. They helped to administer the reward and sanction system for export targets and encourage competition among members through mutual monitoring. The following passage provides a graphic idea of the implementation role of the Korean Traders' Association:

> The head of the export promotion office in the Ministry of Commerce and Industry has at his side a computer printout of progress against targets by industry and by firms. The data is for the preceding day, which is all the more remarkable when it is considered that most developing countries do not have aggregate information on exports for many months.... And in the foyer of the head office of the Korean Traders' Association is a big board tracking the progress of each industry toward its target. The export associations of each industry, the nodes for all information flows on exports, have their own boards tracking progress.[17]

Associations have also helped to implement stabilization efforts both on their own and in concert with government. During the late 1980s, Mexican associations, especially the retailers' association, helped enforce price controls critical to the country's stabilization efforts (Kaufman *et al.*, 1992). Operating within an arrangement known as the Joint Public–Private Consultative Committee, Thailand's peak associations provided the government with information and support useful in Thailand's successful structural adjustment (Doner and Laothamatas, 1994).

Associations can also improve policy implementation by exerting pressure for more regularized administration of functions. In the Thai case, associations have helped to improve customs procedures. In Nigeria, associations in one region effectively opposed 'corrupt behaviour, inefficiency and the politicization of administration' (Lucas, 1993, p. 201). This involved opposition to the state's arbitrary imposition of environmental safety standards and support for improved telephone services. Indeed, according to Lucas, the primary impact of some Nigerian associations may be to force an improvement in the state's basic operating procedures (Lucas, 1993, pp. 220–221).

Finally, associations can affect policy formulation. Such influence can be exerted in countries such as Singapore and Taiwan, where the private sector is clearly subordinate to the state, as well as in countries such as Malaysia and Thailand, where the private sector has more political weight. Associations regularly use their influence to benefit their members at the expense of other groups. What we try to show here is that associations can use their influence for greater social benefit.

In Singapore, the local private sector traditionally had little say concerning the state's manufacturing-based export policy. Indeed, many domestic entrepreneurs have complained that the policy discriminated against them in favour of transnational corporations. But in the mid-1980s, the government reconsidered the pro-TNC, interventionist practices of the past and moved to promote service industries such as finance, transport and communication. Since these are areas in which local firms are relatively strong, the government engaged in unprecedented consultation with the Singapore Manufacturers' Association, the Singapore Federation of Chambers of Commerce and Industry, as well as leading individual capitalists (Rodan, 1993, p. 231).

In Taiwan and Thailand, business associations have used their influence to promote exports. The Taiwan Spinners' Association successfully lobbied the government for low interest loans and simplified tariff collective procedures (subsequently extended to other industries), and pressed state officials to negotiate with the United States on quota issues. If the government dragged its feet, the association sent its lobbying groups abroad independently (Kuo, 1990, p. 108). Thai associations successfully pressed the government to support manufactured exports through more efficient customs procedures and modified tariffs in the late 1970s when the limits of Thailand's economic strategy of import substitution in manufactured goods and export promotion in raw materials were becoming evident (Laothamatas, 1992).

It is also important to note the dynamic nature of associational influence over policy. Here we stress the tendency for growth in associational autonomy, as illustrated in the South Korean case. Cheng argues that South Korea's export-based economic growth has led to a 'pluralization' or equalization of bargaining power between the state and business associations (Cheng, 1988, pp. 26–30). First, the contribution of industrialists and their associations to export growth and thus the country's economic health has strengthened organized capitalists in policy dialogue with state officials. The ability of local capital, including association, to release Korea from an international payments squeeze during the first oil crisis was a critical point in this process.[18] Second, as the limits of state economics control become more obvious and pressures for economic liberalization grow, associations may lose some implementation functions (e.g. import referrals); but they may expand their role in interest representation. Finally, Korean economic growth has enriched business associations, enhanced the organizational resources, and increased their capacity for influence. Here, resources include not only finances but also industrial expertise, information on trade and general economic conditions, and ties to big business overseas. Since the early 1980s, The Korean Chamber of Commerce and Industry has opposed the government on macro-economic policies and the Federation of Korean Industry has challenged state leadership in almost every economic policy area (Cheng, 1988, p. 31).

We have emphasized the economic benefits of active business associations. In so doing, we do not intend to deny that associations often waste resources and sabotage growth by cornering markets, monopolizing licences, buying off state officials and the like. But the less-noticed benefits of associations highlight two important issues: the sometimes beneficial impact of rent seeking and the need for collective action in responding to volatile markets.

Social scientists, especially economists, assume that rent seeking and market domination automatically undermine efficiency and dynamic growth. The Taiwan and Brazilian cases noted earlier suggest that this assumption is not universally valid. Producer cartels established by the Brazilian parts association certainly generated rents for the strongest suppliers. But they also stabilized domestic prices and thereby facilitated exports; and they impeded vertical integration by the assemblers, thereby creating the basis for long-term assembler-supplier linkages and supplier investments and exports with high local value added.

The Taiwan and Brazilian cases also highlight the important (if potential) role of associations in strengthening developing country responses to changing market conditions. Studies of economic governance suggest that where markets are stable and products standardized, producers have modest needs for information. But where demand is constantly shifting, the need for information and other resource flows among interdependent producers intensifies. Business associations can promote and strengthen these exchanges.

Business associations and political development

Organizations influence the ways in which businesses act and the consequences of business actions for political development. Associations can promote political openness, ease the burdens on frail democracies, enhance government effectiveness, weaken anti-democratic alliances, promote political stability, and socialize citizens into democratic behaviour and broader views of group interests. Recent analyses on the transition to democracy have emphasized the importance of various forms of intermediate organization for democratization (Hagopian, 1992; Fox, 1993). While they do not emphasize them, business associations are crucial to the organizational vitality of civil society. Democracy is not fundamentally a question of competition for power among individuals but rather organizations and hence the quality of a society's organizations shapes its political system (Przeworski, 1991).

Associations help make political life more of an open exchange among public and private parties. Organizations collect and process information which can help business aggregate interests and pursue them. Informed organizations, or more specifically their elected leaders, have incentives to be more proactive in anticipating internal conflicts and trying to get business positions on the agenda rather then merely trying to stop or change policies already adopted. Organization gives business a public presence which contrasts with the generally closed nature of patronage networks and gives business an incentive to keep their politics more open (Lucas, 1993, p. 234). Openness and transparency are generally 'public goods' in democracies.[19]

In Mexico prior to the 1970s business associations tried to stay out of politics and government officials strongly encouraged them to stay out. After 1970, relations with the government soured and business sought new and improved organizations, means of dissemination, and ties to political parties. These changes did not lead immediately to democracy, but they did help to open the authoritarian regime, strengthen civil society *vis-à-vis* the state, and swell the ranks of opposition parties (Heredia, 1994).

To the extent that business associations regulate sectors and resolve disputes, they can depoliticize distributional conflict and thereby unburden the political system, with potential benefits for democracy and especially for overburdened young democracies. For example, successful stabilization programmes that minimize social costs often have an incomes policy component requiring concertation among business associations, labour and the state. This pattern was evident in the Thai stabilization efforts during the 1980s, but even more so in neo-corporatist Europe. In Austria and Switzerland peak associations resolved disputes between industries and so 'political conflicts within the business community did not immobilize the public agenda and government machinery' (Katzenstein, 1984, p. 197). Removing the state from wage negotiations is always a boon to the government. Effective centralized employer associations can relieve governments of exclusive responsibility in wage determination in which it cannot please everyone and often pleases no one.

To the extent that democracies are judged on their effectiveness in delivering growth and redistribution, business associations can be key to a favourable rating. Business associations can improve policy in at least three ways. First, associations usually have the capacity to collect and process information that, if properly incorporated into decision making, enhances a range of economic policies. Second, as discussed above, associations can aid in implementing policies adopted by the government thereby enhancing executive capacity. Third, and in part as a result of the better information and implementation, business associations offer governments a wider range of policy options (Atkinson and Coleman, 1989; Streeck and Schmitter, 1985; Schneider, 1993).

Associations can also take pressure off governments by acting as a brake on abuses of power and in some cases taking over state functions. Business associations' efforts to expose and reduce corruption and waste by the Nigerian state may turn out to strengthen the regime's legitimacy by transforming its basic operating procedures.

Associations can anchor or stabilize politics (Streeck and Schmitter, 1985). To the extent that associations have influence they can mitigate sharp swings in democratic and non-democratic regimes. Associations allow for the continuous representation of interests rather than periodic delegation through elections. Moreover, associations provide 'purer' representation of interests. In elections all issues and interests are on the agenda; in lobbying only the affected interests are given voice. The constancy and concentration of interest intermediation by business associations renders their influence more consistent.

Associations can provide business with political 'voice' options that reduce their tendency to link up with other anti-democratic forces. In Latin America democracies have usually ended with coups from the right, led by the military with strong business backing. Based on extensive interview data, Leigh Payne (1994) finds that Brazilian industrialists are perfectly willing to tolerate democracy as long as they feel they have some access and influence (though she implies that business influence is more a function of government receptivity than business organization). Rueschemeyer, Stephens and Stephens (1992) argue that democratic survival in Latin America requires strong right-wing parties that can defend business interests. Strong, effective lobbying associations may keep capitalists away from the barracks by providing them with the capacity to pursue their interests without going outside of or even destroying a democratic political system. The Brazilian parts association constituted one source of opposition to collaborationist leaders supporting the military regime (Addis, 1993).

However, without pro-business parties, the influence of business associations is often dependent on the government. Chilean associations in the 1950s and 1960s gained institutionalized influence through various business–government commissions and formal participation in other policy and legislating agencies (Menges, 1966; Stallings, 1978, pp. 34–41). They subsequently lost influence in the Allende government and ultimately supported its overthrow. Thailand has exhibited a similar pattern: associations gained influence through state-backed Joint Public–Private Sector Committees but have continually lacked ties to political parties. With the demise of government backing for the JPPCCs in the late 1980s, associational influence dwindled rapidly.

Several of the potential contributions of associations noted above to democracy and stability in fact detract from purer or more naive principles of democratic governance. Unburdening the polity by depoliticizing distributional conflict also puts an essential struggle in all capitalist societies beyond the reach of democratic institutions. Stabilizing the political system implies attenuating politicians' electoral mandates. Guaranteeing business influence in policy making means limiting the influence of other social groups (that usually represent larger numbers of voters). These are core concerns in any society. The dilemma of balancing economic inequality with political equality confronts all capitalist democracies. Our concerns are more immediate and pragmatic. Given the poor survival rate of democracies in developing countries, the first order of business is minimal consolidation. In this, business associations can help them in the short run be more governable and stable, and less vulnerable.

Business associations may also perform Tocquevillean functions. Intermediate organizations such as business associations may be vehicles for channelling the participation of business elites in political life and for expanding the purview of regional or ethnic-based business interests.[20] For businessmen in Northern Mexico, participation in business associations was often a trigger for their entry into opposition politics. Manuel Clouthier was the president of several associations before becoming the candidate for the PAN in the 1988 elections. Fernando Clariond and Rogelio Garza Sada, from the firms and families of the group of 10 in Monterrey, both claimed that the experience of association politics had driven them into opposition politics, again in the Partido de Accion Nacional.[21] Several Thai businessmen became cabinet members in the late 1970s after having developed contacts and policy positions as association leaders. Again, however, the extent of such political socialization seems to depend on the stability of linkages to political parties.

Finally, business associations can encourage entrepreneurs to go beyond narrow views of economic interests. One pattern of such broadening is seen in Africa where the elaborate network of patronage connections between state and capital have traditionally led to what Richard Sklar has termed a 'political' rather than 'economic' capitalist class. In Nigeria, business associations have promoted an entrepreneurial identity more distinct from those controlling political resources (Lucas, 1993, p. 233). A second pattern involves the transcendence of community identity such as ethnicity or geographical base. Although such identities are often critical bases of initial associational strength, they can undermine national integration and exacerbate political cleavages. It is clear that business associations in South East Asia have been important channels for inter-ethnic linkages and ethnic assimilation.

Explaining differences in business organization

The primary purpose of this chapter has been to consider the ways in which business associations contribute to democracy and development. Nonetheless, given our conclusion that these associations matter, it is worth considering, at least briefly, why it is that the extent and strength of business organization varies so much cross-nationally. We consider a number of possible influences, beginning with a group of socio-economic variables.

The size and economic capacity of the indigenous business class might constitute a background or threshold variable: as complexity increases, informal communication becomes less effective, making it more likely (but not necessarily) that an association will emerge. We are not looking for a one-to-one correspondence but rather merely noting that business associations are unlikely to emerge before large groups of managers and owners exist. While good comparative data on the number, diversity, and budgets of associations are lacking, it seems that the more industrialized countries of Latin America and Asia have more numerous, more specialized, and richer associations than do the poorer countries of Africa and Latin America.

Ascriptive linkages promote associational activity by reducing free riding and the transaction costs necessary for organization. This appears to be the case in South East Asia, but in Latin America immigrant status seems to have dampened activity in business associations. Part of the explanation for the difference may be due to the fact that immigrant businessmen in Asia are predominantly Chinese, whereas, in Latin America they came from a variety of different European and Middle Eastern societies.[22]

The vulnerability of an economy to external shocks influences the incentives to organize and seems to explain a lot of cross-national variations. Business in the smaller more trade dependent economies of Europe is generally well organized (Katzenstein, 1984). In Latin America many of the earliest associations were founded and dominated by domestic agricultural exporters such as coffee growers in Colombia, Costa Rica and

Brazil, and wheat and cattle producers in Argentine (where exports were controlled by multinational companies the organizing impulse was weaker). The depression hit the liberal exporting countries of Latin America especially hard and triggered a wave of defensive business organizing. This general economic shock was especially important in promoting cross-sectoral organization, as in the (state chartered) industrial associations of Brazil and Mexico, and the Chilean peak association, the first in Latin America, founded in 1935. In the case of manufactured exports later in the twentieth century, the incentive to organize was often weaker where states mediated international shocks.

The preceding socio-economic factors constitute underlying causes or permissive variables. Political factors act as more proximate, precipitating agents. Where state intervention in the economy is widespread, detailed, and discretionary, the incentives for collective action are low. When middle level officials decide price controls, loans, import licensing, etc., businesses have a primary interest in developing close, personalistic ties to the bureaucracy, rather than investing in collective action. Moreover, in authoritarian governments suspicious of autonomous organization, officials can withhold subsidies to undermine collective action.

Where authority over economic policy is highly centralized within the state, business associations tend toward comparable (isomorphic) centralization (Nordlinger, 1981; Skocpol, 1985). Both states and peak associations are centralized in Japan, Korea, France, and to a lesser extent Mexico (after 1975). Government fragmentation, as in the United States or Brazil, encourages fragmentation business associations as differing factions attempt to weigh in at one or another veto points, and centralized peak associations are feeble at best. These variations are most apparent in cross-national comparisons. There may also be a similar though less pronounced effect over time. Thai peak associations were stronger in the 1980s when they faced a relatively centralized state but became more fragmented with the subsequent transition to a more fragmented government.[23] There are exceptions to this isomorphism. For example, Mexico (before 1970) and Taiwan had relatively centralized states, but the peak associations of business were weak or non-existent. Other factors, such as ethnic cleavages in Taiwan, or regional diversity and corporatist prohibitions against peak associations in Mexico, can suppress organizational isomorphism.

Major political and economic crises are often foundational moments for business associations. As noted, business in Latin America experienced a wave of organization in the 1930s under state corporatist auspices. State elites were wary of these new associations and often struck corporatist deals in which business organizers ceded some controls on their organization in return for a state solution to their free-rider problems – compulsory membership. Later in the post-war period threats from the left provided renewed motivations to organize. In Latin America, a widespread perception of immanent threat to property rights swept away barriers to collective action (Payne, 1994). Often the barriers re-emerge immediately after the threat passes, as in Brazil after the military coup of 1964, though in other cases the incipient organization survives and thrives, as in Mexico after Echeveria when the Business Co-ordinating Council (CCE in Spanish) gained organizational force.

The most proximate cause for variations in business associations is direct state intervention in organization through either legislation or the formal or informal provision of benefits to associations and their members. Most governments in Latin America in the 1930s and 1940s adopted legislation governing the terms and conditions under which labour and business could organize. In Japan for most of this century officials have encouraged various sectors to organize and then made the new associations the privileged intermediaries in policy implementation. In other countries the state has formally devolved public functions such as worker training, setting product standards, and allocating export quotas to associations. In all these instances direct state intervention was the decisive factor in determining variations in activities and organization (as discussed earlier).

Much of the variation in the organization of business can be explained by the more structural variables analysed above, though other residual factors, such as leadership, should not be ignored. While the organization of business in Brazil was until recently largely the result of state corporatism, early organization owed a great deal to one industrialist, Roberto Simonsen, who invested heavily in organizing in Sao Paulo and nationally and who influenced the way the government implemented its plans for state corporatism. Overall though, the ability of business leaders to solve their own collective action problems is limited in the absence of government support and/or favourable socio-economic factors.

Summary and conclusion

This chapter represents a distillation of a growing literature on the potential contributions of business associations to political and economic progress in developing countries. The initial approach was deliberately inductive as we sought first concrete examples of positive contributions rather than deductive principles. Ultimately our goal is to match this empirical material with middle range theoretical propositions that would elaborate and synthesize recent theoretical developments in the study of institutions (particularly the new institutionalism in sociology, political science, and economics), economic governance, and meso-corporatism.

As a first step the key dimensions of variation were identified. Associations pursue an analytically distinct yet empirically mixed set of activities that follow the logics of membership or governance, influence, and implementation. Associations vary in their willingness and ability to fulfil these logics in part because their internal organization is so varied. Business associations vary in terms of the scope and density of their membership, their organizational resources, and their power over their members. The identification of these core dimensions does not provide an exhaustive list but rather the beginnings of a more parsimonious set of variables that are causally related to the positive outcomes covered subsequently in the chapter. Winnowing the field of candidates is a preliminary step in constructing a framework for comparative analysis.

The next step was to concentrate on the governance functions of associations that provide collective goods otherwise underprovided by the market. These collective goods included a full range of business services as well as the resolution of conflicts between upstream and downstream producers. We then turned to the political contributions associations can make, such as unburdening the government and depoliticizing explosive distributional conflicts through associations' governance and implementation activities. Influence activities were more important in promoting political stability and inhibiting the formation of anti-democratic coalitions.

Our comparative survey turned up a wide range of variation in the activities and origins of business associations. This range suggests that associations are malleable and can be fashioned to serve a variety of purposes. This range also suggests caution in attempting to extrapolate from the US experience (a generally negative view) or the European experience (a more positive perspective).

We have emphasized the potentially positive impacts of business associations: but experience suggests that these institutions are schools for corruption and strategic advantage in the tradition of Olsonian distributive coalitions as often as they are schools for democracy and transaction costs economizing in the tradition of encompassing, productive coalitions. Indeed, some research suggests that they are often both, depending on the context. A major task is therefore to identify the factors influencing associations in one direction or the other.

What makes associations use their political influence, market power, and rents in socially beneficial (if not necessarily optimal) ways? Our analysis suggests three possible causes. A first organizational variable, scope, determines the way interests are aggregated, integrated, and reconciled. In particular, where peak associations have coercive powers over members they can force members to resolve disputes and seek common ground, which is likely to be closer to a position of greater general welfare.

Second, export markets seem to provide discipline or disincentives for collusion. For example, upstream and downstream producers can resolve disputes through associations in efficient and therefore socially beneficial ways, not because they are encompassing or altruistic, but rather because they must succeed in export markets. Associations born out of vulnerability to external markets (and without recourse to state protection) may have an organizational bias to socially beneficial collective action, even in the absence of immediate market discipline.

Third, states may discipline business associations. Interventionist states that cede benefits or authority to business associations can use the threat of withdrawal as a significant incentive for associations not to abuse their powers. Since association leaders know members belong largely because the association has the state concession, the leaders will not want to jeopardize the concession. However, effective discipline may require a rare kind of state that is sufficiently insulated and autonomous to withstand counter pressures from associations seeking particular advantage.

Business associations in Europe are often largest and most influential in wage negotiations. This function is largely absent from our survey because unions have been weak and repressed and employers' associations are consequently weak or non-existent. If democratization and industrialization foster stronger unions, this function could well become more important. Moreover, as redistributive issues climb the agenda past growth, as in the Asian NICs and Chile, this function may be key to both future growth and political stability.

The challenges of successful integration into volatile and competitive international markets may in the future require governance structures different from those at the vanguard of development in the past. That is, statist promotion of Fordist industries may not be sufficiently responsive, varied, and flexible to launch industries into changing market niches. More fluid and decentralized governance, led by business associations, may provide superior solutions.

Lastly, and most generally, developing countries are characterized by a lack of institutions of all sorts: parties, associations, state bureaucracies, representative bodies, unions, and markets. Building successful capitalist democracies requires progress on all fronts over the longer term. However, in the short run when urgency is greatest, some institutions may be easier to strengthen and may serve as short-term substitutes for others. For example, markets, parties, and public bureaucracies usually require generations of institutional building (Huntingdon, 1968; Evans, 1992). Streeck and Schmitter (1985) argued that associations could complement and compensate for the inevitable failures of markets and states. The implied assumption in their argument is that societies may tend toward an optimal balance among the various forms of institutions. This may well be the trend at high levels of development. For poor countries the more interesting question is whether or not there is a grey zone in the intersections of markets, states, and associations where institutions are fungible and substitutes.[24] If so, associations might provide partial institutional substitutes while societies work through more intractable problems in building states and markets.

Notes

1. This chapter draws on unpublished work by Doner and Wilson. Ben Schneider thanks CIS at Princeton and the Kellogg Institute at the University of Notre Dame for their support.
2. Schmitter, forthcoming. Governance can also be understood as the 'totality of institutional arrangements – including rules and rule-making agents – that co-ordinate and regulate transactions inside and across the boundaries of an economic system'. (Streeck *et al.*, forthcoming). See also a similar definition by Williamson (1985, p. 41).
3. We define a sector as a group of firms defined by the production of 'actually competing or potentially substitutable products'. (Schmitter, forthcoming, p. 22.) Note, however, that governance structures exist not only among these core firms but also between them and a number of other environments. The latter range from upstream suppliers of raw materials, components, machine tools, to downstream distribution networks and customers, to bankers, venture capitalists and shareholders. See also Streeck *et al.*, forthcoming, p. 8.
4. During the 1950s and 1960s, modernization theory did generate studies of intermediate organizations in Latin America based on the premise that societies generate associations as they modernize. Elsewhere, however, modernizations theory emphasized the backward nature of local capital and the danger that interest groups and their representatives might overload delicate political systems. Dependency theory also kept business associations in the background. For some, the dominance by foreign capital made local associations irrelevant. Even studies that focused more on the role of local capitalists neglected the ways in which they organized. (Cardoso and Falletto, 1979; Evans, 1979; Becker, 1983). Statist writings, at least in their initial stages, shared dependency's assumptions that in their initial stages, shared dependency's assumptions that developing country entrepreneurs were weak and short-sighted.
5. This argument is drawn from Streeck and Schmitter (1985, pp. 3, 4).
6. 'Logics' of membership and influence are drawn from the work of Streeck and Schmitter (1985).
7. Our review of organizational variation is not exhaustive. Our intent was to cover the dimensions that have the greatest impact on the capacity of associations to fulfil one or more of the three logics. A full review would also consider the nature of membership (individuals, firms or associations), representation (voting by member, dues paid, number of workers, or other measures of size), and regional versus sectoral representation in peak associations.
8. Generally the proportion of firms or individuals in the association is a less relevant measure of density, except in the case of organizations of small and

medium business where the strength is in numbers of people rather than economic weight.

9. Information on Korean associations is drawn from Cheng (1988, p. 22). This unpublished work remains one of the most thoughtful pieces on business associations in the developing world.
10. Encompassing organizations do not benefit when any one sector or group gains rents (Olson, 1982, p. 48). However, encompassing organizations were not a major concern for Olson since according to the logic of collective action small groups would be more successful in overcoming barriers to collective action and their interests would necessarily be particular and damaging to overall efficiency. Moreover, Olson was sceptical about encompassing organizations because they tend to reduce competition if strong but are generally too weak to restrain their members from seeking particular benefits to the detriment of overall social welfare (Olson, 1982, pp. 50, 52).
11. Offe claims that organizations of employers and investors (in contrast) 'do not generate power that does not already exist, nor do they formulate ends that do not derive directly from the ends that are already defined and consciously pursued at the level of the individual members firms' (Offe, 1981, p. 148).
12. The major industry association in Sao Paulo (Veja) spent nearly $500 million on training in 1992. See Weinstein (1990) for history.
13. For more on the success of governance under Japan Spinners' Association in reducing capacity and modernizing the industry in the 1960s and 1970s, see McNamara (1993).
14. Author interviews.
15. Interview with Raul Ortega, COECE, November 1993.
16. Discussion of the export roles of Korean associations is drawn from Cheng (1988, pp. 14–16).
17. Rhee *et al.* (1984) p. 22, cited in Rodrik (1993), p. 14.
18. One contribution involved the Federation of Korean Industries co-ordination of Korean construction firms' business in the oil dollar rich Middle East (Cheng, 1988, p. 28).
19. In some cases high profile organization may be disadvantageous in that it arouses opposition and suspicion. In Brazil, business lobbies were considered illegitimate during the 1946–64 democracy and business kept a low profile (see Leff, 1968). Organization may also be dangerous in places such as Indonesia and other countries where minority entrepreneurs seek to downplay their economic strength.
20. Business associations might also function as 'schools of democracy' linking traditional and modern social systems. Based on our knowledge, such a pattern seems to be weak at best. It does occur to some degree among associations in Thailand, especially among those outside Bangkok (Laothamatas, 1992). But in the Nigerian groups studied by Lucas, associational life mirrored the non-participatory tendencies seen more generally in Nigeria: few meetings were held and most decisions were made by leaders with no consultations. Since incumbents were never challenged, the lack of electoral competition may have reinforced autocratic practices (Lucas, 1993, p. 204).
21. Interviews conducted in November 1993.

22. In Mexico, for example, immigrant entrepreneurs were more likely to 'confine their role mainly to company interests', and not to take a broader social view of their firm or to engage in public activities (Derossi, 1971, p. 191).
23. British and American businesses were much more organized during the mobilization for the two world wars.
24. Laothamatas (1992, p. 169) argues that strong business associations (and the Thai model of development) are good for other developing countries that cannot create hard states like those in Taiwan and Korea.

APPENDICES

Spain – a passive business actor

Alfredo Pastor Bodmer and
Jordi Solé Tristán

The Spanish 'transition to democracy' began in 1975 with the death of General Franco, and culminated three years later in the approval by national referendum of a constitution which established a parliamentary democracy. This transition took place peacefully, through institutional reform of the authoritarian regime of General Franco. The fact that in only a few years the Spanish institutions created under Francoism evolved towards the typical models of a modern parliamentary democracy in a peaceful way, can only be understood if the following factors are taken into account:

- The collective national memory of the tragic end to Spain's first democratic experience in the twentieth century – the Second Republic, from 1931 to 1939 – which ended after a three-year-long civil war. In the collective imagination the damage caused by this civil war was estimated to be a million deaths. The refusal to repeat such a tragic experience no doubt conditioned the attitudes of all the protagonists of the democratic transition.
- The rapid economic development promoted during the second half of Franco's reign, and the enormous socio-economic changes it brought about.
- The designation in 1969 of Prince Juan Carlos as official successor to General Franco as head of state. Politically this decision prevented a vacuum of power and the consequent political instability which would have been inevitable if the appointment of a new head of state had been left in the hands of a series of high-level official organisms without any real legitimacy.

- The growth, diversification, professionalization and rationalization of the civil service, coupled with its growing autonomy from the political rulers.
- The depoliticization of the armed forces, and their subjection to political control.
- The supremacy of a centralized and disciplined army over the country, and the lack of any armed opposition.
- The organizational weakness and political division of the democratic opposition to the regime.

Throughout the modernization process of the 1960s and 1970s, and the subsequent democratic transition, business played an exceptionally passive role:

- At no stage did the business sector assume a leadership role on issues of economic development, the liberalization of markets, or the democratization of the country.
- Throughout the Franco period, business did not attempt to create any independent organizations to defend their short- or long term interests. In a sense, business delegated to others – the state and the Catholic Church – the defence of its interests in the short and long term. Its political, social and economic position during the transition was extremely fragile.
- It is noticeable that as the Francoist regime liberalized, trade unions seized and created the space to create their own autonomous organizations, but the business sector did not. By 1975 independent working-class trade unions had become a powerful social force, despite having been outlawed and persecuted by the Francoist state, while business forces still had no organization to defend their interests.
- The Spanish entrepreneurial class only existed as a lobby for its own narrow interests. Thus it lobbied for privileges, import barriers, etc. This combination of social passivity and lobbying activity gave rise to an extremely negative image of Spanish businessmen. As a result of this passivity, the political, social and economic position of the business sector during the transition to democracy was extremely fragile, and there was an almost total lack of communication between business and politicians. The passive role that Spanish businessmen played in the capitalist modernization of the country, and the image of them as an excessively accommodationist and privileged group which was conveyed to society in general, or which they allowed to be conveyed, might have been one of the causes of the lack of communication between them and the politicians. Interestingly, the democratic politicians have a favourable attitude to foreign businesses, which are seen as the harbingers of progress, efficiency and modernity.
- In the present democracy, as under Franco, the most frequent complaint

of businessmen is and has been that the politicians do not know what a business is, are not aware of the problems of business, and are only interested in macro-economic theory and issues. They say there is an almost total lack of communication between business and politicians.

- Until 1978 business did not manage to create a national organization for the defence of its interests against trade union organizations or the state. And only after 1978 did other business organizations begin to appear whose aim was the legitimation of the role of business in society (such as the Business Circle, the Institute of Family Businesses, the Association for the Advancement of Managers, the Institute for Economic Studies, etc.).
- The only business group that created an organization independent of the corporate syndical organization formed and controlled by the state was the banking interests. However, even this sector was only interested in obtaining privileges from the politicians, and it too was simply a lobby.
- The fact that the banking establishment was the only organized business group with influence over political power is seen as a key reason why the economic language used by the Spanish political class – under Franco and under democracy – was and has been basically macro-economic, and therefore quite distant from the problems of businesses. Most officials holding economic ministerial posts under Francoism and under democracy have spent some time during their previous professional careers in research departments of one bank or another.

It seems fair to conclude that the lack of interest by business in issues beyond its own economic concerns has been an important factor in the continuing failure to establish a common language and value system shared by businessmen and politicians in both Francoist and democratic Spain.

The fact that business in Spain did not play an active role in the capitalist and democratic transitions should not be taken to mean that such a role by business is either irrelevant or incidental to a successful transition.

In Spain this vacuum was filled by the Catholic Church – especially its religious orders, and specialized secular organizations – which played a critical role in both types of transition. This activity included running the country's oldest and best management and engineering schools, providing protection to workers' unions or modernizing politicians, and playing a key role in devising state reform strategies.

Business in Indonesia – a vulnerable actor

Robert W. Hefner

Over the past 25 years, Indonesia has gone from being one of the world's poorest nations to the threshold of becoming one of South East Asia's industrializing giants. Today, Indonesia has a growing economy, a healthy industrial sector, a modest but growing middle class, and a larger and more assertive business community than at any time since independence from the Dutch in 1949.

Despite the historic weakness of the Indonesian business community, recent events have placed statist politicians on the defensive and strengthened the hand of those committed to export-oriented industrialization under the direction of, above all, private enterprise. For the first time in modern Indonesian history, a substantial private sector and non-governmental middle class are taking shape, and pressures are mounting for economic and political liberalization. Yet, despite these developments, the long-term role of business and its impact on the broader political scene remains uncertain and will be determined by the interplay between government, business and society.

Business associations have begun to exercise a measure of influence over economic policy, but Indonesian political life remains tightly controlled. The only business associations tolerated by the government are those it sponsors and whose directors it approves. As a result, business inputs on economic policy tend to be limited to specific economic matters, not general concerns. Although the private sector has come to be regarded as an important engine of economic growth, there remain in Indonesian society and government influential social groupings opposed to market-oriented growth and in favour of a strong, state-led process of industrialization.

The Indonesian example provides several important lessons for the comparative analysis of private enterprise, development and democracy. Most generally, Indonesia serves as a sobering reminder of the complexity of state–business interactions in much of Asia, and the difficulties involved in speaking of business as a social grouping or class always distinct from the state. As in many other parts of developing Asia, and, for that matter, the non-Western world, historically the role of the business community in Indonesia has been far more circumscribed than that of business and, more generally, the urban middle class or bourgeoisie of Western Europe and the United States. For most of the independence period, the Indonesian business community has not been an independent social group distinct from the state, but has been strongly tied to the government elite through a complex network of cross-cutting memberships, political patronage, and state-promoted corporatist organizations. The relationship of business and government in Indonesia reminds us that, rather than being typical, the peculiar autonomy that business and the enterprise-oriented middle class achieved in the West is really quite unusual.

The vulnerability of the business community to outside political control has been exacerbated by the fact that about two-thirds of mid- and large-scale private enterprise in Indonesia has been owned by Chinese Indonesians. Chinese comprise just 3 per cent of the country's population. Though some among the Chinese minority immigrated to the archipelago centuries ago, most Indonesians regard the Chinese as non-'indigenous'. Despite their economic importance, the Chinese are marginalized from formal politics and regarded with resentment by many native or pribumi Indonesians. Their dominance in the marketplace is also deeply resented by much of the native population. At various points in Indonesian history, governments have exploited this ethnic antagonism to put pressures on the Chinese and exact payments from them, and conversely to use the Chinese as a foil against the development of a native business community that might challenge state power. If government policies are seen to reinforce Chinese dominance, the business community will remain divided and the prospects for further reform will diminish.

In modern Indonesia, the continuing vulnerability of what is in fact the most economically dynamic segment of Indonesian business has undercut the business community's ability to assert any kind of collective social programme, or to promote such general concerns as the rule of law, protection of property rights, and the right of non-governmental actors to be heard by policy makers. It has thereby undermined its ability to exercise a liberalizing influence over Indonesian government and society.

Although analysts of capitalist development in East Asia have sometimes seen 'state insulation' from organized interests in society as an important variable in the equation for economic success, in Indonesia the insulation of the state from societal pressures has included its insulation from business leaders and liberal advisers hoping to encourage a greater measure of market discipline. In the 1980s, some business associations in Indonesia began to influence economic policy, but that influence was largely restricted to micro-economic policy, and even then operated on only a few specific manufacturing domains. Input from business associations varies according to industry, and tends to be weakest in spheres where the vested interests of high-ranking government officials and their well-connected business allies are strongest.

The complexity of business–government alliances in Indonesia requires that we be careful not to conceptualize either 'business' or 'the state' in terms based on prototypes derived from Western political history, where the autonomy of the business community from the state was considerably greater than is the case in Indonesia, or, for that matter, other parts of developing Asia. Business and government are not neatly polarized or mutually distinct. Some businessmen advocate greater business autonomy and transparency; but others are closely linked to high-ranking officials, in relationships that vary from pure rent-seeking to business partnerships. These divisions within the business community have limited its ability to influence economic policy, regularize market relations, and in Gordon Redding's apt phrase in this volume, 'thicken' civil society.

Business in the Philippines – a self-conscious business actor

Bernardo M. Villegas

In 1970 the leading large businesses in the Philippines established an organization called Philippine Business for Social Progress. Contributing 1 per cent of their annual net profit to a common fund, more than 100 firms sought to combat mass poverty by pooling their resources and efforts into such areas as low-cost housing, co-operative development, assistance to small- and medium-scale industries, and the development of the most depressed regions.

The record of the business community, at various times, has been both as an outspoken critic against tyranny and a vigorous and patient advocate of peaceful change in the transition to and consolidation of democracy in the Philippines. This Philippine Business for Social Progress has stated:

> The business of private enterprise must not only be business, but also the building of an enterprise on social development. In short, the new enterprise of private enterprise is social development; the business of business is the development of man.

Filipino industrialists have also been at the forefront of social reform by teaming up with the Bishops of the Catholic Church in the Bishops Businessmen's Conference for Human Development (BBC), organized in the early 1970s. They felt: 'The key to social development is not in providing the poor with free services, but in making the poor productive.' Through this forum, some of the leading business people actively pushed for reforms that were initially unpalatable to their business and political colleagues, such as agrarian reform, the banning of log exports (a most ecologically damaging industry), and minimum wage legislation.

It was also an initiative of some enlightened members of the business community that led to the establishment of a privately funded business and economic think-tank, the Centre for Research and Communication (CRC), in 1967. The CRC's mission was to help members of the Philippine business community transcend their narrow individual interests by working for causes that promote the common good of society. For 25 years, the CRC oriented its research and communication programmes towards following this path. In time, this think-tank became the ally of the Makati Business Club (an influential group of businessmen who speak out on political and economic issues), providing socio-economic information to corporate executives in efforts to move the country towards a more market-friendly and democratic dispensation.

The acute political and economic crises of the 1980s spawned favourable conditions for even greater activism of the business sector in the economic development and democratization of Philippine society. Business actions helped to secure the peaceful transition to democracy, and are currently designed to help consolidate democratic institutions and processes. This included:

- greater involvement in socio-political affairs by the Bishops Businessmen's Conference (consultations between BBC and leaders of the peasantry, fisherfolk, labour, and the urban poor have resulted in the Social Pact alliance) and the Makati Business Club;
- the establishment of the National Movement for Free Elections (NAMFREL) – which plays a continuing role in facilitating and ensuring free, fair and efficient elections at all levels of government – was a landmark in the history of the political involvement of the business sector;
- numerous non-governmental organizations have been established or reinvigorated by businessmen to fill the void left by a generally weak, inept and corrupt government bureaucracy. It is very revealing that many international aid agencies prefer to channel funds to these business-related non-governmental organizations, including the Philippine Centre for Investigative Journalism (reform of the media); Philippine Business for Social Progress (countryside development, and regional dispersal of economic opportunities); the Dualtech Foundation (the training of industrial workers); Philippine Business for the Environment (sustainable development); the Fund for Private Education (education reforms); Project Congresswatch (monitors Congress, fosters public accountability promotes transparency of elected officials, educates citizens on the work of Congress, teaching participants how to determine whether the promises of their representatives square with their performance); Project Courtwatch (examines court activities, procedures and case loads through a system of selective observation); and the Foundation for Judicial Excellence (created by business

executives and lawyers to foster judicial excellence by evaluating the performance of judges).

Another key NGO is the business-assisted Asian Free Trade Commission, designed to combat the remaining vested interests supporting protectionism, and opposing the liberalization and deregulation of the economy.

The administration of Corazon Aquino was a great victory for the business sector clamouring for greater participation. President Aquino reminded the business community that greater participation implied greater responsibility and a keener sense of the common good. She loosened the business environment by opening up the economy. Her government undertook trade reforms, passed the Foreign Investment Act, and took initial steps of financial and foreign exchange liberalization, among others. Through the years even before her rise to power, such entities as the CRC were already pushing for the same reforms. Their activities conditioned a large segment of the business community to accept some painful reforms that would prove to be beneficial in the long run. Today, pressing for people empowerment and global competitiveness as the keys to national development, President Ramos is continuing in the footsteps of his predecessor in liberalizing the economy. A substantial segment of the business community supports him.

The business community in the Philippines today sees itself as the primary actor in economic development, with the government playing a supportive but minimal role. As a businessman has put it: 'We view our role as basically an engine of growth for the economy. Our strength lies in our ability to mobilize resources, make investments and create jobs.'

The vigour of the business community in undertaking non-traditional activities within society introduces a whole new dimension to its role as the engine of development in Philippine society. In developing countries, where the state lacks the resources to single-handedly lift the poor out of their condition, the business sector serves as an intermediate institution that can supplement the efforts of the state or even become the main promoter of the development of the poor.

The prospects are bright for a more positive and proactive role for the Philippine business sector in the economic development and increased democratization of Philippine society. The restoration of democracy has not meant the end of the involvement of business in politics. Their efforts today are focused on fortifying democratic institutions and propagating democratic processes. Subjects of business concern for democratic consolidation range from the judiciary and the legislature to elections, political stability, and the peace process. At the end of the day, the greatest contribution of businessmen to economic development and democratization is still their willingness to operate within a truly competitive market economy.

Government and business in contemporary Mexico

Carlos Elizondo and Blanca Heredia

Business has long held a pivotal position in Mexico. Over the last decade the economic as well as the political centrality of private economic elites has experienced a formidable leap. This heightened centrality is the result of two main factors. The first is long-term domestic and international shifts, both of which have steadily increased the weight and importance of private capital in the structure and operation of the Mexican economy. The structural position of business in a capitalist economy has provided and continues to provide Mexican business people with the key instrument through which to limit the state's ability to employ its power against it. The second is the introduction, beginning in the mid-1980s, of a series of major reform initiatives that have greatly expanded the role and scope of private choices and market forces in the management of economic life.

Mexico is formally a democracy. It has regular elections, a party system, an elected president, and an elected Congress. In practice, however, one party has dominated political life since 1929. The hegemonic position of the Partido Revolucionario Institucional (PRI) in Mexican politics has been, to a large extent, based upon the corporatist arrangement created in the aftermath of the 1910 revolution. An extremely strong presidency and the official party remain the anchors of the political system.

As a group, businessmen have not been active in either the PRI or in opposition parties. The dispute about political power has not historically been their central concern. Moreover, despite certain common interests, cleavages existed within the business community which severely limited its capacity to directly shape economic reforms, and means that the ability of business to influence events is unequally distributed. Some sectors, for example highly mobile finance, are much more powerful and influential than others, such as industrialists with high sunk costs. Influence also varies depending on the policy issue concerned and appears to be greater in the overall framework than in specific arenas. This has to do with the essentially negative quality of the power that business has. Its ability to veto continues to be far greater than its capacity to participate actively in the definition of policy and, more importantly, to assume a positive role in Mexican politics.

There are two major confederations of business chambers, affiliation to which is mandatory: CONCAMIN (National Confederation of Industrial Chambers) that represents industrialists; and CONCANACO (National Confederation of Commerce Chambers), most of whose members are merchants, but businessmen in industries such as tourism and restaurants are also included. CONCAMIN has usually been on good terms with government. The nature of industrial activity in Mexico, long dependent upon protection, trade preferences, special credits, and vulnerable to both tax auditing and strikes, helps explain this. CANACINTRA (National Chamber of Manufacturers) is an important and very large industrial chamber, which is formally associated with CONCAMIN. CANACINTRA acts as the representative of those firms whose development and success has been most directly dependent on government protection and had traditionally provided, as a result, government's firmest support within the private sector.

CONCANACO, organized on a regional basis, tends to be more autonomous *vis-à-vis* government, at both federal and regional level. Its independence is the result of the commercial and service firms' greater economic autonomy. Merchants can and have been affected by government-imposed price controls. Such controls, however, cannot be targeted against individual merchants; only against particular products.

Certain voluntary business associations have been created to defend specific interests, or in response to perceived threatening government policies. The most independent and vocal opponent within the private sector is COPARMEX (National Employers' Confederation), whose approximately 30 000 voluntary members tend to be more active and committed to it than CONCANACO and CONCAMIN affiliates. One of the most influential private sector associations is the Mexican Council of Businessmen (CMHN), a group of 30 leading businessmen. It was founded in 1962 in reaction to President Lopez Mateos's left-leaning economic and social policies. The Council's strength rests on the economic weight of its individual members as well as upon their traditionally close personal ties with top government officials, including the president himself. The structure and operation of the CMHN exemplifies in many ways the basic nature of the relationship between government and the private sector: it usually follows a low-profile strategy, and its regular meetings with the government tend to be conducted in secrecy.

In 1975 an umbrella organization, the Business Co-ordinator Council (CCE) emerged in response to President Luis Echeverria's populist policies. It serves as a unifying framework for major business organizations, including the two mandatory ones, CONCAMIN and CONCANACO.

The creation of CCE marked an important shift in business–government relations. For the first time, businessmen were endowed with a unifying vehicle through which to confront government. The CCE is not formally recognized by the government as a legal organ for consultation with the private sector, but it has become a key player in practice. Its participation in the introduction and continued operation of a tripartite arrangement involving business, labour and government in a concerted effort to bring down inflation has greatly reinforced its position.

The position of business within Mexican society is a peculiar one. At least until the 1970s, businessmen had what they needed, namely important channels of communication and access to those areas of policy-making that affected them. These channels were severely damaged during the Echeverria administration and during the last year of Lopez Portillo's government (1976–1982), when government intervened in ways that could be construed by private investors as threatening. In the latter half of 1982 everything seemed to coalesce so as to make confrontation between Mexican business and the authoritarian régime certain. An economic crisis of major proportions – GNP experienced a negative growth rate of −0.5 per cent, inflation reached 98.9 per cent, the value of the peso was devalued by 466 per cent, the government increased its foreign debt by almost six billion dollars – severe divisions within the regime, erratic decision-making, and attacks against business could not but generate widespread anti-government reactions on the part of the private sector. Capital flight reached unprecedented levels. Investment stopped. Anti-government press campaigns, both inside and outside Mexico, proliferated. Public demonstrations in favour of democracy were staged by major business leaders and organizations, and private entrepreneurs began to swell the ranks of the Partido Action Nacional. The intensity of the confrontation between business and government, along with the rapid politicization of important segments of the Mexican private sector during the early 1980s, were quite unprecedented. In contrast to most other authoritarian regimes in the region, conflict in state–business relations stopped short of rupture and the political activation of business failed either to facilitate or directly contribute to a full-fledged transition to democracy.

Privileged access and close ties were re-established in the second half of de la Madrid's administration (1982–1988), and consolidated in the course of the Salinas one.

Upon assuming office, de la Madrid was forced to deal with an economic crisis of major proportions and to do so having to face an unprecedentedly recalcitrant and politically active private sector. He actively attempted to re-establish communication with major business elites, and managed to do so relatively quickly through both political and economic means. The structure that facilitated *rapprochement* between government and business was the CMHN, whose informal and closed character was useful in that it allowed the government to re-establish contact with these groups outside the larger, more public and highly politicized private sector organizations such as the CCE, CONCANACO and COPARMEX. The crisis in government–business relations was reversed. The need to regain business confidence and to deactivate the politicization of growing segments of the business community forced government to engineer a far-reaching shift in favour of the market.

However, the government's ability to reconstruct an alliance with the dominant economic elites did not simply entail a return to the *status quo ante* of 1970. Not only had the economy experienced major transformations; Mexican society and business itself had also undergone major changes. In spite of the growing *rapprochement* between government and the dominant economic elites, and in sharp contrast with the past, important segments of the Mexican business community continued to engage in an unprecedentedly diverse range of political and civic activities throughout the 1980s. Active and unusually open involvement in partisan politics in civil associations of various sorts, as well as in cultural, educational and philanthropic endeavours, continued to expand, primarily from the ranks of medium-sized entrepreneurs. Business people's participation in electoral contests – particularly at the regional level – grew rather than abated.

For business people the real risk of a democratic transition remains whether or not it endangers the governability of the country. If the transition proceeds smoothly, business people are unlikely to oppose it. The problem is that governability at present is more difficult to obtain than in the past. The constraints imposed by the need to consider the interests and demands of big business place considerable burdens on the capacity of the regime to cope with pressures from below. Paradoxically, the situation is one in which the structural power of capital may well limit the ability of government to ensure social and political stability.

Business in Nigeria

Adebayo O. Olukoshi

Since the early 1980s a growing interest in the role of private business in the processes of economic development and political change in Africa has emerged. This interest has been in the context of the adoption by many countries on the continent of structural adjustment economic reforms and multiparty political forms. Nigeria, with one of the biggest private sectors in Africa, has witnessed a slow process whereby business, initially profiting from state protectionism and interventionism, was later to push vigorously for economic deregulation and the rolling back of the state.

Nigeria's business sector is complex in composition, and spans various spheres of economic activity. Made up of indigenous Nigerian, Levantine, Indian and Euro-American businessmen and women, the Nigerian business community also consists of traders, manufacturers, bankers, insurers, commercial farmers, owners of mines, building contractors, shippers, airline operators and hoteliers, among others. The business concerns over which they preside are overwhelmingly concentrated in the medium-scale category, employing between 100 and 500 workers. Furthermore, most of the businesses, especially the manufacturing enterprises, are located in the consumer goods sector. The state itself is an important player in the business sector, not just as a regulator but also as an owner and operator of business assets through its host of enterprises, parastatals and public corporations. Indeed, given the resources it controls, it can be argued that the state is the single biggest actor in the Nigerian economy and this is a position it has maintained in spite of the attempts at rolling back its frontiers as part of the structural adjustment process.

The economic role of the state for the private business sector in the country is important. The origins of the pre-eminent role of the state in Nigeria's economic affairs are inseparable from the history of development of capitalism in the country. What this implied was that, from the outset, business depended on access to the state for its survival and reproduction. Although, over the years, many a business group attempted to establish some autonomy from the state in the conduct of their activities by tapping a local mass market or serving other private sector groups, not all were able successfully to define their objectives independent of the vagaries of state policy. The onset of the Nigerian oil boom of the early 1970s and early 1980s was in fact to confer even more influence on the state as it received and controlled the disbursement of well over 90 per cent of all foreign exchange receipts accruing to what is a heavily import-dependent country. Access to the state was, therefore, critical to business; and as a means of ensuring this, a significant number of enterprises, both indigenous and foreign-owned, had joint partnerships of some sort with the state at a time when the oil boom strengthened the nationalist impulse in the country.

Given this, it should not be surprising that the distinction between public and private business in Nigeria is not a very sharp one. Both the public and private sector interpenetrate one another. Many private sector operatives are not only part of joint ventures with the state, but also depend on state orders and contracts for their reproduction. A significant number sit on boards of public enterprises and parastatals. Many in the business sector look up to the state to give a lead in matters of economic and social development. Clearly, the Nigerian private business sector cannot fruitfully be understood independent of its dialectical relationship with the public sector. Precisely because of this relationship, which in its workings is both collaborative and conflictual, the private business sector has a direct stake in questions of state power and policy direction. The way in which it chooses to develop that stake is, in our view, partly a function of the nature of the business class and the dominant thrust of its activities. In Nigeria, the dominant thrust in the business class is clearly compradorial.

Business hardly took an active, direct interest in national politics during the colonial period and after independence until very recently. Although business responded to the emergence and growth of nationalist politics in Nigeria after 1945, it did not make major contributions to the struggle for independence. Business groups, however, took steps to prepare themselves for the demands of independence. But organizations of business, such as the chambers of commerce, shunned party politics, as did most members of the business community. This was so in spite of the growth of patronage in the state allocation of resources as well as the many inconsistencies in economic policy caused by the dynamics of party (and later military) politics, the rapid turnover of regimes, and the acute political instability of the country. What most members of the business community did was not to seek collectively to strengthen their own lobby to obtain consistency in governmental policy, but rather to plug individually into the patronage networks that proliferated in order to have access to foreign exchange and other resources provided by the state. This was so until the early 1980s when, following an economic crisis, business began to make spirited efforts to address the problems of politically motivated resource allocation that had become dysfunctional and which the import licensing rackets of the Nigerian Second Republic (1979–1983) brought out vividly. Major changes began to occur in the perceptions of business with regard to the management of the country's resources and politics.

The introduction in 1986 of an International Monetary Fund/World Bank-sanctioned structural adjustment programmeme (SAP) was not only partly an outcome of pressure mounted by business but also raised hope in the most influential business circles that the significance of patronage politics, which heightened disillusionment with state interventionism, would decline sharply. However, the failure of SAP to achieve its objectives even as patronage politics flowered in spite of economic deregulation soon led to profound disillusionment in the private sector, especially among manufacturers, who increasingly made a linkage between economic management and the country's political regime. Business organized itself with a view to directly influencing the state's record of economic management, as well as governmental transparency and accountability.

It was the failure of structural adjustment to achieve its objectives or to supplant, even subordinate, patronage politics that brought business into the arena of the national quest for political change. As noted earlier, prior to the 1980s business hardly concerned itself with politics as a group, though individual businessmen and women were either active in party politics or plugged into state economic interests with the country's political fortunes more actively following the political crisis which was created by the annulment of the June 1993 elections by the military regime of General Ibrahim Babangida.

In economic as in political matters, business was to find itself in an uneasy alliance with a broad coalition of forces, such as labour, students, professionals and academics who were in the front-line of opposition to structural adjustment as practised by the military and the perpetuation of the Babangida dictatorship in the political arena. In order to ensure that the government improved its poor record of economic management, business made direct representations to it, holding pre- and post-budgetary meetings with top-level state officials, insisting on strict budgetary monitoring, and participating in an economic summit hosted by the state. At the political level, business contributed to the quest for political reforms through such organizations as the Concerned Professionals.

Overall, business as an actor has, over the years, gradually become involved in broad social, political, and economic concerns. It can be argued that although business has made increased progress in promoting political and economic change, including on its own terrain and in the wider society, there is no doubt that considerable room for improvement exists all round. Business has to develop and strengthen its enlightened self-interest in such a way as to combine its particular objectives with a social responsibility that will enable it to play a relevant and meaningful role in the country's political and economic development. Part of the strategy for achieving this will have to include an active dialogue, not just with the state but with other social actors in Nigeria.

Business in Atlanta – the city too busy to hate

Laura L. Nash

Atlanta is one of the few US cities to achieve real economic growth among a widespread black and white constituency since the election of its first black mayor, Maynard Jackson, in 1973. Under 25 years of black control of City Hall, Atlanta has experienced an economic boom while maintaining an active and diverse political power structure. Though the city's economic and democratic progress is not an unqualified success, Atlanta has none the less been unusual in its ability to enlarge both the political and economic prospects of its citizenry. Atlanta's business community – white and African-American – has been a key factor in this city's progress.

As a sign of its power as a civic entity, Atlanta has seen a general increase in national and international stature, evidenced not only by its choice as the site of the 1994 Super Bowl and the 1996 Summer Olympics, but in Atlanta's regular appearance on lists of the top 10 best cities to live in.

From the 1940s, Atlanta's governance structure was historically centred on a small group of white businessmen who headed the city's largest downtown businesses. Largely through private friendships and other informal mechanisms, they shaped a progressive, economically ambitious plan for Atlanta's expansion. This group controlled the choice of mayor and was a buffer between more racist white businessmen and the black community. Black interests were represented by a network of middle class professionals who negotiated directly with the white business elite, rather like a patron–client relationship.

As federal civil rights removed the last legal barriers to discrimination, this balance of power shifted, with the black community increasingly using economic coercion to achieve desegregation and greater economic and educational opportunity. In the 1973 election for mayor, blacks had a voting majority for the first time, and Maynard Jackson, an African-American from Atlanta, was elected mayor. The business elite no longer controlled City Hall. The mayor, however, had little control over investment in the city.

Rather than destroy each other in a bid to capture power, these two groups created a new power coalition under which business and City Hall were able to advance their agendas. Subsequent mayoralties (Andrew Young, then again Maynard Jackson) have cemented this power regime. During these past 25 years, Atlanta has experienced an economic boom, increasing the growth of the black middle class, but also increasing poverty rates.

A productive relationship between Atlanta's largest firms and the new City Hall was established, which affected economic development. The business group was not indifferent to the fortunes of the city and, taking a strong lead from the chairman of Coca-Cola and his friends, was particularly adept at taking a unified stand in order to get things done. An ethos of consolidated economic growth and personal citizenship permeated their decisions.

The largest corporations, such as Coke, BellSouth (with the support of the United Communications Workers) and Georgia Power, made a visible commitment to affirmative action programmes, and clearly were aware of the need for good public relations in this area. They were also concerned to set a precedent, knowing that the courts would continue to back desegregation.

It must also be understood that the pro-business attitude of City Hall was a key factor in the successful integration of business's strategy. The mayors were also adept at knowing how to use the idea that development could not afford escalations of racial tensions to secure co-operation at times of greatest opposition from business. Five other factors were crucial to the success of the business community's ability to both continue to shape the city's economic agenda and be responsive to democratic demands from City Hall for increased minority contracting and jobs. These factors are:

- a cosmopolitan vision of the city that thought big, underlying a long-term economic strategy that 'fits' with the predominant business ethos;
- an acute self-consciousness about 'image', and an ability to market image successfully;
- a small, efficient business elite composed of 'upstarts', supplemented by a black elite network;
- strong educational institutions in the black and white communities; and
- a highly diversified but complementary industry mix concentrating on service industries with an international/global focus.

Without denying that today's problems may require totally new approaches than those of the past, it is none the less instructive to reiterate the unique combination of strengths that the Atlanta business community brought to the issue of desegregation. The business elite was able to shape and sell a vision of growth that was consistent with more inclusive civic values and anticipated a globalized service economy. It put the real forces of image and reputation to economic and democratic good use. Far from being a showpiece of buyout, the business group alliances have effected a partial democratization of the business community's own power structure, and are seen to have been the key vehicle for introducing important new democratizing agendas into Atlanta's civic progress.

Bibliography

Addis, C. (1993) Local models: auto parts firms and industrialization in Brazil, PhD dissertation. MIT, Department of Political Science.

Atkinson, M. and Coleman, W. (1989) Strong states and weak states: sectoral policy networks in advanced capitalist economics, *British Journal of Political Sciences,* **19**(1), pp. 47–68.

Bartell, E. and Payne, L. (1994) *Business and Democracy in Latin America.* Pittsburgh: University of Pittsburgh Press.

Becker, D. (1983) *The New Bourgeoisie and the Limits of Dependency.* Princeton: Princeton University Press.

Bhagwati, J. (1993) *India in Transition: Freeing the Economy.* Oxford: Clarendon Press.

Bielschowsky, R. (1988) *Pensamento Economico Brasileiro: O Ciclo Idologico do Desenvolvimentisomo.* Rio de Janeiro: IPEA.

Boisot, M. and Child, J. (1988) The iron law of fiefs: bureaucratic failure and the problem of governance in the Chinese system reforms, *Administrative Science Quarterly,* **33**(4), pp. 507–527.

Booth, A. (1992) *The Oil Boom and After.* Singapore: Oxford University Press.

Bruton, H.J. (1992) *The Political Economy of Poverty, Equity and Growth.* Published for the World Bank, Washington, DC: Oxford University Press.

Cardoso, F.H. and Falletto, E. (1979), *Dependency and Development in Latin America.* Berkeley: University of California Press.

Cheng, T. (1988) Business interests associations in export oriented industrializing economies: theoretical observations and a Korean case study. Paper presented at the 1988 meeting of the APSA, Washington, DC, 5 September.

China Securities Regulatory Commission/The Stock Exchange of Hong Kong Ltd. (CSRC/SEHK) (1993) *A Practical Guide to Listing: Papers Presented at the Share-Issuing Seminar Beijing,* September 1992, Hong Kong.

Derossi, F. (1971) *The Mexican Entrepeneur.* Paris: OECD.

Diamond, L. (1988) Democracy in Africa. In L. Diamond, J.J. Linz and S.M. Lipset (eds), *Democracy in Developing Countries.* Boulder, CO: Lynne Rienner.

Doner R.F. (1992) Limits of state strength: toward an institutionalist view of economic development, *World Politics,* **44** (April), pp. 398–431.

Doner, R.F. and Ramsay, A. (1993) Economic growth and public–private sector relations: the case of Thailand. Paper presented at the Workshop on the Role of Collaboration Between Business and the State in Rapid Growth on the Periphery. Princeton, NJ.

Doner, R.F. and Laothamatas, A. (1994) Thailand: economic and political gradualism. In S. Haggard and S.B. Webb (eds), *Voting for Reform: Democracy, Political Liberalization and Economic Adjustment.* New York: Oxford University Press/World Bank, pp. 411–452.

Evans, P. (1992) *Dependent Development: the Alliance of Multinational, State, and Local Capital in Brazil.* Princeton: Princeton University Press.

Faaland, J., Parkinson, J.R. and Saniman, R. (1990) *Growth and Ethnic Inequality: Malaysia's New Economic Policy.* London: Hurst and Company.

Fox, J. (1993) The difficult transition from clientelism to citizenship: lessons from Mexico, *World Politics,* **46**(2) (January), pp. 151–185.

Frankel, F.R. (1978) *India's Political Economy, 1947–1977. The Gradual Revolution.* Princeton: Princeton University Press.

Gellner, E. (1992) *Reason and Culture.* Oxford: Blackwell.

Gold, T. (1996) Civil society in Taiwan: the Confucian dimension. In W.M. Tu (ed.), *Confucian Traditions in East Asian Modernity.* Cambridge MA: Harvard University Press, pp. 244–258.

Hagopian, F. (1992) Democracy in developing countries: Latin America, *World Politics,* **45**(3), pp. 464–501.

Heredia, B. (1994) Mexican business and the state: the political economy of a 'muddled' transition. In E. Bartell and L. Payne (eds), *Business and Democracy in Latin America.* Pittsburgh: University of Pittsburgh Press.

Hirschman, A. (1973) The changing tolerance for income inequality in the course of economic development, *Quarterly Journal of Economics,* **87**(4), pp. 544–566.

Hollingsworth, J.R. and Streeck, W. (eds) (forthcoming) *The Governance of Capitalist Economies.* Oxford: Oxford University Press.

Horowitz, D.L. (1985) *Ethnic Groups in Conflict.* Berkeley: University of California Press.

Huntington, S. (1968) *Political Order in Changing Societies.* Newhaven: Yale University Press.

Jesudason, J.V. (1989) *Ethnicity and the Economy: The State, Chinese Business, and Multinationals in Malaysia.* Oxford: Oxford University Press.

Katzenstein, P.J. (1984) *Corporatism and Change.* Ithaca: Cornell University Press.

Kaufman, R., Bazdresch, C. and Heredia, B. (1992) The politics of economic reform in Mexico: the solidarity pact of 1987–88. Papers on Latin America No. 28. Columbia University.

Knight, J. (1992) *Institutions and Social Conflict.* New York: Cambridge University Press.

Kochanek, S.A. (1974) *Business and Politics in India.* Berkeley: University of California Press.

Kotkin, J. (1993) *Tribes: How Race, Religion and Identity Determine Success in the New Global Economy.* New York: Random House.

Kuo, Cheng Tian (1990) Economic regimes and national performance in the world economy: Taiwan and the Philippines. PhD dissertation. University of Chicago.

LaNoue, G.R. (1992) Split visions: minority business set-asides, *The Annals of the American Academy of Political and Social Science*, September, **523**, pp. 104–116.
Laothamatas, A. (1992) *Business Associations and the New Political Economy of Thailand*. Boulder: Westview.
Leff, N.H. (1968) *Economic Policy-Making and Development in Brazil 1947–1964*. New York: John Wiley.
Lim, F.D. (1989) Channel for community, *Far Eastern Economic Review*, 23 Febıuary, p. 7.
Lucas, P.J. (1993) State and society in Nigeria: a study of business associations in Kano. PhD dissertation. Indiana University, Department of Political Science.
MacIntyre, A. (1991) *Business and Politics in Indonesia*. Sidney: Allen and Unwin.
McCormick, B.L., Su, S.Z and. Xiao, X.M (1993) The 1989 democracy movement: a review of the prospects of civil society in China, *Pacific Affairs*, **12**(1), pp. 28–41.
McNamara, D. (1993) Association and adjustment in Japan's textile industry, *Pacific Affairs*, **66**(2), pp. 206–209.
Menges, C.C. (1966) Public policy and organized business in Chile, *Journal of International Affairs*, **20**(2), pp. 343–365.
Moon, C. and Prasad, R. (1993) Beyond the developmental state: institutions, networks, and politics. Paper presented at the annual meeting of the American Political Science Association, Washington, DC, 2–5 September.
Nordlinger, E.A. (1981) *On the Autonomy of the Democratic State*. Cambridge: Harvard University Press.
Offe, C. (1981) The attribution of public status to interest groups. In S. Berger (ed.), *Organizing Interests in Western Europe*. Cambridge: Cambridge University Press.
Olson, M. (1982) *The Rise and Decline of Nations: Economic Growth, Stagflation, and Social Rigidities*. New Haven: Yale University Press.
Papanek, G. (1967) *Pakistan's Development: Social Goals and Private Incentives*. Cambridge: Harvard University Press.
Papanek, G. (1986) *Development Strategy, Growth, Equity and the Political Process in Southern Asia*. Pakistan Institute of Development Economics.
Papanek, G. (1988) The new Asian capitalism: an economic portrait. In P.L. Berger and Hein-Huang Michael Hsiao (eds), *In Search of an East Asian Development Model*. Rutgers University Press. (Transaction Books).
Papanek, G. (1989) Growth, poverty and real wages in labour abundant countries. Background Paper for The World Bank *World Development Report* 1990. (Unpublished).
Payne, L. (1994) *Brazilian Industrialists and Democratic Change*. Baltimore: Johns Hopkins University Press.
Piore, M.J. and Sabel, C. (1984) *The Second Industrial Divide: Possibilities for Prosperity*. New York: Basic Books.
Przeworski, A. (1991) *Democracy and the Market: Political and Economic Reforms in Eastern Europe and Latin America*. Cambridge: Cambridge University Press.
Puthucheary, M. (1993) Malaysia: safeguarding the Malays and the interests of other communities, *Democracy and Development*, September, **6**, pp. 23–40.
Rhee, Y.W., Ross-Larson, B. and Pursell, G. (1984) *Korea's Competitive Edge: Managing the Entry into World Markets*. Baltimore: Johns Hopkins University Press.

Rodan, G. (1993) Reconstructing divisions of labour: Singapore's new regional emphasis. In R. Higgott, R. Leaver and J. Ravenhill (eds), *Pacific Economic Relations in the 1990s: Cooperation or Conflict.* Boulder: Lynne Rienner.

Rodrik, D. (1993) Taking trade serious: export subsidization as a case study in state capabilities. Paper presented at the Conference on New Directions in Trade Theory. Ann Arbor, 29–30 October.

Rowe, W.T. (1990) The public sphere in modern China, *Modern China* **16**(3), pp. 309–329.

Rueschemeyer, D., Stephens, E.H. and Stephens, J.D. (1992) *Capitalist Development and Democracy.* Chicago: University of Chicago Press.

Schmitter, P.C. (1971) *Interest Conflict and Political Change in Brazil.* Stanford: Stanford University Press.

Schmitter, P.C. (forthcoming). Comparing the institutions of modern capitalism: sectors, their governance and performance. In J. Hollingsworth and W. Streeck (eds), *The Governance of Capitalist Economies.* Oxford: Oxford University Press.

Schneider, B.R. (1993) The elusive embrace: collaboration between business and the state in developing countries. Paper presented at a conference on Relations between Business and the State in Developing Countries. Princeton: Princeton University Press.

Skocpol, T. (1985) Bringing the state back in: strategies of analysis in current research. In P.B. Evans, D. Rueschemeyer and T. Skocpol (eds), *Bringing the State Back In.* New York: Cambridge University Press.

Snodgrass, D.R. (1980) *Inequality and Economic Development in Malaysia.* Oxford: Oxford University Press.

Sowell, T. (1993) Middleman minorities, *The American Enterprise,* May–June, **4**(3), pp. 30–41.

Stallings, B. (1978) *Class Conflict and Economic Development in Chile, 1958–1973.* Stanford: Stanford University Press.

Streeck, W. and Schmitter, P.C. (1985) *Private Interest Government: Beyond Market and State.* London: Sage.

Streeck W., Hollingsworth, J.R. and Schmitter, P.C. (forthcoming). Capitalism, sectors, institutions and performance. In J. Hollingsworth and W. Streeck (eds), *The Governance of Capitalist Economies.* Oxford: Oxford University Press.

Wade, R. (1990) *Governing the Market: Economic Theory and the Role of Government in East Asian Industrialization.* Princeton: Princeton University Press.

Wakeman, F. (1992) *Did China ever have a civil society?* Public lecture. University of Hong Kong.

Weiner, M. (1978) *Sons of the Soil: Migration and Ethnic Conflict in India.* Princeton: Princeton University Press.

Weinstein, B. (1990) The industrialists, the state, and the issues of worker training and social services in Brazil, 1930–50, *Hispanic American Historical Review* **70**(3), pp. 379–404.

Williamson, O. (1985) *The Economic Institutions of Capitalism.* New York: Free Press.

World Bank (1990) Poverty: World Development Report 1990. Oxford University Press.

World Bank (forthcoming) Levels of spatial coordination and the embeddedness of institutions. In J. Hollingsworth and W. Streeck (eds), *The Governance of Capitalist Economies.* Oxford: Oxford University Press.

Index